ANYTHING
for a
LAUGH

ANYTHING
for a
LAUGH

Memoirs

ERIC
NICOL

HARBOUR PUBLISHING

Harbour Publishing
P.O. Box 219
Madeira Park, BC V0N 2H0 Canada

Cover design, page design and composition by
Martin Nichols, Lionheart Graphics
Cover illustration by Peter Lynde
Photograph credits: BCBW—BC BookWorld; UBC—University of British Columbia Library; Special Collections.
All other photographs from Eric Nicol's collection.

We acknowledge the financial support of the Government of Canada through the Book Publishing Industry Development Program and the Province of British Columbia through the British Columbia Arts Council for our publishing activities.

Printed and bound in Canada.

Canadian Cataloguing in Publication Data

Nicol, Eric, 1919-
    Anything for a laugh

    ISBN 1-55017-187-9

    1. Nicol, Eric, 1919- 2. Humorists, Canadian—Biography
    I. Title.

PS8527.135Z53 1998   C818'.5403   C98-910644-6
PR9199.3.N5Z463 1998

THE CANADA COUNCIL | LE CONSEIL DES ARTS
FOR THE ARTS | DU CANADA
SINCE 1957 | DEPUIS 1957

For
Cathy, Claire and Christopher,
the important issue

YIPPEE-YI ... OH

Whoop-up westerner through and through,
I clapped my spurs to the wooden steed
of a carousel career,
mistook my mount's ups and downs
for galloping to glory,
missed the brass ring by a finger,
and now that the merry-
go-round's
stopped,
I wander anxious to the exit,
looking for my mummy.

Contents

Introduction

A Disclaimer

What *are* memoirs? Laundered biography? The alcoholic's remembrance of times pissed? The last ego trip into the sunset of a career? Or just a way to scratch out a few more bucks before God closes the account?

Whatever. What's for sure is that no one *asked* me to write these memoirs. It was my own idea. I have no excuse for exposing myself in print. After all, I do own an old raincoat.

Also, I have no claim to fame. I have not achieved celebrity in politics, sport, movies or war—the certified justification for writing an autobiography as other than a private catharsis, like picking one's nose. I have never lived with chimps in the jungle, or created a diet program that lets you eat anything but your spouse, or worked as a happy hooker (unless you count my teaching Creative Writing 100, living on the avails of prose tuition).

No, the main reason for my writing this book was to get my life off my chest. To put my past on paper. The paper is recyclable. My past, probably not.

Nearly everyone, as he or she gets older, has this urge to throw up his memoirs. The vanity press thrives on that compulsion. But I vigorously deny that the small print of the contract for this book includes my having to mow the publisher's lawn.

Another statement that I'd like you to believe: this autobiography is not one of the great love stories of our time. Much as I'd like to come across as lovable as George Burns, I am not old enough. An entry-level human being: that is the best rating I can hope for from the reader, the impression being improved by my emerging as a modest fellow. I am very proud of my modesty. Indeed, I am willing to stack my diffidence up against that of anybody in my weight class. *False* modesty? Maybe. But the teeth are still mine.

So, given the limitations of a life not notable for chutzpah or other stimulants, what does this book have to offer to the reader besides a place to park his brew and spare the coffee table? What interest lies in an old white male whose spirit of adventure has rarely ventured beyond raking leaves in a strong wind, a person who can boast of pioneering no new frontier of sexual intercourse, someone whose love life has, in fact, been gravely impaired by fear of consequences? In short, sort of a nonmalignant lump.

Well, first of all, I'd like to dispute the belief that the professional humorist is dead. I say that I am still alive. The reader may want to ask for a second opinion. But even if I am wrong, I think it important to speak up, from the grave if necessary, to encourage young people to make fools of themselves in print, where there is less chance of contracting a sexually transmitted disease.

Second, and as a more general raison d'être for this auto-biography, I hope to demonstrate that today's kids have more in common with my generation—prehistoric though it may seem—than with the intervening Me Generation, Whee Generation, HIV Generation.

For instance, sexual abstinence is reported to be in vogue among teenagers. To wait is cool. This may be a marginal movement among our youth, but it so happens that I wrote the book on deferred deflowering. I am something of a role model for the innocent who may overdo it.

From experience, or the lack of it—whichever came first—I know that it isn't easy for a young man to say no to sex. *But it can be done.* Yes, kids, and you will be glad you postponed a pleasure that for girls, especially, is rarely unmitigated.

The restraint starts with eating your piece of pie from the crust forward, leaving the best for the last. Of course, a lot depends on whether your date looks as good as a pizza.

Finally I should admit that more things happened to me in my life—lay or spiritual—than are chronicled in this account. Some of them may have been quite important. Like my losing my virginity. I have no recollection of where I lost it. I may have just mislaid it. Sometimes I think I still have it, until I remember I apparently fathered three children.

If it *is* possible to impregnate a woman while remaining chaste, I've probably done it. I don't remember.

Let's face it: I am mentally handicapped. Having a bad memory for names, in particular, has meant that I live in ter-ror of meeting an old girlfriend in the supermarket, someone with whom I have been intimate, and having to greet her with, "Hi, there!"

One of the reasons I enjoyed writing stage plays was that I could call everybody "darling." Both genders. A real godsend to the absent mind.

In school I had to develop a photographic memory for exam purposes. My brain was one big darkroom. But after someone let the light in, my memory faded faster than a hooker's smile.

However, writing memoirs with a lousy memory is akin to making a cake with no flour. You really have to lean on the icing. I envy the great memoirists who have benefitted from having total recall. I have only partial recall. That is, I'm apt to remember what I've been partial to, such as blondes, and forget the rest.

For the reader, though, the upside is that I shall not be name-dropping as much as I would if I could remember names to drop. Also, my editor has warned me that if I do drop a name, I had better have had more to do with that famous person than to ask for an autograph. For instance, I was once a member of a press scrum that interviewed Marilyn Monroe on the occasion of her materializing in Vancouver. But I never lined up with the Kennedys to sleep with her, or even had my photo taken with Marilyn sharing an airport. So that's it for Marilyn Monroe.

Given these parameters, I guess the only justification for my helping to deplete Canada's forests with this book, is that it may encourage other nameless people to experience the catharsis of writing their own memoirs, even though they remember little and were never groped by President Bill Clinton.

Please forgive the occasional attempts to climb up on a soapbox that could have been a high-rise but for the vigilance of my editor, Michael Carroll.

Welcome to my life!

Chapter 1

Derivation

During my formative years (1919–1998), I was attracted to both academia and competitive sport. I attribute this genetic ambivalence to my grandfather, Patrick Mannock, who was *the* teacher of billiards in turn-of-the-century England. I never met him, my mother having run away from home as a teenager, never to be reconciled with her parents. My main source of information about my Irish grandfather has been his obituary in the *Times* of London, circa 1934:

> The death of John Patrick Mannock, aged 73, took place at his home at 25 Park-avenue, Church End, Finchley, N. London recently.
>
> Mannock, one of the greatest billiards coaches in the world, had been teaching at Burroughs and Watts Hall, London, until shortly before his death.
>
> Mr. Mannock taught the game of billiards to

many famous men, and his pupils included King Edward, when Prince of Wales, Lord Oxford and Asquith, Sir Arthur Conan Doyle, Sir Thomas Lipton, Sir Hugh Hurst and Marchese Marconi.

When a schoolboy, Mr. Mannock often met Charles Dickens, and he delighted in relating the story of how he was taken to see him by his father, a great friend of the novelist, and given a penny many times.

He wrote "Billiards Expounded," a classic of the game, which earned the commendation of Sir Thomas Lipton.

Mr. Mannock was an uncle of Major R.E. Mannock of the Royal Air Force who in 1918 won the Victoria Cross.

Mrs. W. Nicol, of 4027 West Sixteenth, Vancouver, is a daughter of J.P. Mannock. The noted billiards pioneer was a native of Dublin.

I have ever remained in awe of this bit of ancestry, especially since I learned billiards in a common hotel, self-taught. I have tried to flesh out this sketchy acquaintance with Grandpa Mannock—owner of literally plush billiards parlours in London and Cambridge—by fantasizing the scene of his trying to teach the bibulous Edward VII, who was not noted for his attention span, the rationale behind striking the ball with the lesser end of the billiards cue.

"Congratulations, Your Highness! Your ball remained on the table this time! Now, if you can contrive to make the white ball cause the red ball to enter the pocket."

"Don't be absurd, Mannock. Members of the royal family never put *anything* in the pocket."

Similarly my perception of Sherlock Holmes is coloured

Grandpa Mannock, billiards minister to the Crown, c. 1910.

by knowing that his creator was assisted by my maternal grandfather in solving the mystery of the Green Cushion. Unfortunately, despite the Marconi connection, I still don't understand the wireless.

But as a career guideline drawn in blood, which was more relevant for J.P. Mannock's grandson: that he had written a classic book that has been holy writ for generations of Minnesota Fatses, or that I, too, was blessed with good hand-eye coordination? High school didn't clarify this dichotomy for me—I wrote for the *Scarlet and Grey* student paper, and won my big block as school Ping-Pong champ. Mixed message.

I have since gleaned a report that the great-grandfather who took a junior J.P. to meet friend Charles Dickens was a distinguished London newspaper editor. If true, this would account for the printer's ink in my veins, in lieu of something that might have made me tall enough to play in the NBA.

Anyway, from Grandpa Mannock I never heard a word. My mother was not only the black sheep of the family, but she had strayed into the wilds of a colony—Vancouver, British Columbia. I was, therefore, a bewildered kid when the obituary notice came from my mother's aunt in the Old Country...and she cried all day.

"I thought you didn't like him," I said by way of consolation.

Eyes reddened by grief, she replied, "You don't understand."

Indeed, I didn't.

What I *did* know about my mother was that she was a rebel. This made life difficult for me as a teenager. My own rebellion had been preempted by Mom. Good old Mom, who rolled her stockings, wore high heels to make breakfast and smoked like an Italian volcano, to which she was not so distantly related. A hard act to follow, as a revolter, without appearing derivative. To this day, I have never smoked a cigarette, or got drunk, or worn very short skirts.

My flaming youth had the pilot light snuffed. I blame my mother.

Her story, probably sanitized in the recounting to me, was that after the J.P. Mannocks became the parents of Amelia (my mother) on November 2, 1895, they waited fifteen years

Mom (standing at back) *with the twin reasons why she ran away from home, c. 1910.*

before bearing twins (Ralph and Enid). Amelia was assigned to perambulating the postscripts around Regent's Park, and to baby-sit while the billiards master and his lady sipped Lipton's tea with Sir Thomas. When Amelia slashed the tires on the baby buggy (or the Edwardian equivalent), her parents dispatched her to a convent school in Belgium, praying for redemption. My mother told me gleeful stories of how she organized the other girls to steal food from the holy pantry after lights-out, and hold nightie parties while the mother superior slumbered.

My mother's conduct was so disruptive that the convent obliged her parents to repatriate her before she became a serious threat to Roman Catholicism. From her Continental experience Amelia gained a smattering of colourful French phrases and a strong distaste for organized religion. I was raised as a devout heathen.

As a terrorist, my mother's familial credentials were impressive. Her cousin, Major "Mick" Mannock, V.C., D.S.O. (three times), M.C. (twice), was recognized by the British Air Ministry to have been the most devastating Allied air fighter of World War I, with seventy-three kills verified. He was shot down in flames, and killed, just before the war ended. I have studied a photo of that ruthless hunter of the Hun, and have seen in his dark eyes the same fiery spirit as shone in those of the raven-tressed beauty that was my mother in her girlhood portrait of her family.

Besides this ferocious Celtic strain that her father had mercifully sublimated by shooting down billiard balls, Amelia had genes inherited from her mother, who was half-French, half-Italian, my maternal great-grandfather having been a Count di Negri of Genoa, who reputedly fought beside Garibaldi in the Italian wars of independence. My mother's middle name was Camille, but she was a *dame aux camellias* in whose veins ran the stuff of heroes.

Luckily for little old mongrel me—since I have never had any real aspiration to die young though gloriously—my mother married an Englishman. At least I got the impression that William Nicol was English, despite the Scottish ancestry of the clan Nicol. I once visited a Scottish tartan-cloth factory in Forfar to try to trace my name's legitimacy. I was shown the Nicholson tartan and was assured by the resident genealogist that the clan was an offshoot of the Highlander Argyles, and that I had every right to wear gaudy socks.

The one person I could *not* ask about my surname was Pop. It was tacitly understood in our family threesome that one did not discuss my mother's parents, because she hated them, nor my father's parents, because he was some kind of orphan of the storm.

I doubt that any family has had so little discussion of forebears. Only after my parents died was I emboldened to piece together the family coat of arms: a question mark rampant on a field of London fog.

Documented by their marriage certificate is that my father was born in Edmonton (the original) on August 17, 1892. In his unfinished autobiography, "To Whom It May Concern," he says that his boyhood home was at 5 Bowes Road, New Southgate, North London.

"I remember very little of my childhood," he writes, "except I did very well at the local LLC school and I played on the soccer team. I also started work at Victors Grocery store, and worked many hours a week for very little pay…. My duties were serving customers, delivering groceries far and wide and preparing dried fruits for the store…."

No mention of parents. It was an Uncle Ernest who took up the collection to ship William to Canada, aboard a steamer crammed with poor immigrants.

"The stench below decks [was] unbearable," writes my father. "Besides cattle, the cargo consisted of a large number of Russians (men and women) [who] lived on black bread which they carried in sacks. The bread was very hard, so the only way to feed the children was to soften the bread in their mouths, and transfer it to the children...."

Bill Nicol arrived in Montreal on May 6, 1906: "I was then fourteen years old, and for all intents and purposes alone in the world."

Thus, both of my parents were teenage waifs, one a refugee from a gilded cage, the other from the almshouse. Maybe that is why they worked so hard to give me a compatible home until I was thirty-five.

Chapter 2

What I Owe Kaiser Bill

More or less sold into slavery in Northern Ontario, my father was one of the land kids exported to Canada in the first decade of the 1900s. Exploited by unscrupulous farmers, sheltered warmly by others, often sleeping in haystacks or grain bins, he moved cheerfully from job to job, supported by a sturdy physique, as far west as Saskatchewan. He did a stint in Oshawa, affixing metal braces to buggy seats at the McLaughlin Carriage Works (later part of General Motors), where he began his lifelong, if doomed, love affair with the automobile.

The handsome young stud worked in Toronto in 1914 as a movie extra in a film called *On the King's Highway*, which was being shot at Casa Loma. He was attending a merry cast party at the Canadian National Exhibition when a recruiting sergeant, on the prowl for cannon fodder to feed Canada's entry into World War I, strolled into the bacchanal cow barn. A few months later Pop was on a troop ship dodging submarines, en route to Blighty.

Because he had taken a quickie course in accounting during a lull between harvesting on the Prairies and deck-handing on Great Lakes grain ships, Bill was quickly designated as Staff Quarter Master Sergeant Nicol in charge of stores for his company. And it came to pass, while he was stationed at Witley, Surrey, that the lusty, vagabond jack-of-all-trades crossed paths with the beautiful daughter of England's grand bey of billiards, thus creating the main drag of my conception.

Amelia, aka Millie, had found asylum with her Aunt Maddie, who owned a hat shop. She earned her keep by modelling hats and serving customers. She later denied that this included setting her cap for my father, insisting that SQMS Nicol blandished her with crown roasts of beef scrounged from the army stores over which he held absolute command. It appears, therefore, that I may owe my existence to a wartime shortage of meat in Britain. As Billie plied Millie with necklaces of plump sausage, with ruby solitaire chop, her resistance waned. The natty uniform, plus the prime source of protein, won her heart.

Equally binding was their delight in entertaining, via the concert parties that were the main means of relieving boredom for the troops in the huge training camp at Witley. Miss Mannock, whose graces included playing the piano, provided accompaniment for a comedy routine entitled "The Country Curate" that Sergeant Nicol had worked up. During his peregrinations around Canada, he had joined whatever local church was the socially liveliest, becoming a Methodist in Northern Ontario, an Anglican in Oshawa and a Presbyterian on the Prairies.

This eclectic role in church activities gave him a unique opportunity to observe preachers without being unduly distracted by the sermon. Hence the skit that he and my mother performed for years, long after the war, for Canadian Legion dinners and house parties where, parked in a bedroom with the coats and hats, I became conditioned to adjoining roars of laughter at my parents' contribution to sanctified burlesque: "In our parish news, Mrs. Bumley had the misfortune to encounter a swarm of bees, and was stung on the way to the station." (Roar of laughter.) "There was a large gathering there." (Another roar of laughter.)

My father clipped episcopal gags from wherever he read them, and by the time I was ten he had perfected fifteen minutes of tight, surefire material accented by his curate's hat, by pince-nez perched on his naturally ruddy nose and by furious mugging guaranteed to make his audience pee their pews.

This religious experience pretty well ruined Sunday school for me. I kept waiting for the punch line. My parents once enlisted me in a Bible class, but soon extracted me after pleas by the teacher, who was unnerved by my sitting there with an expectant grin on my face.

Among my father's effects, after he died at age eighty-five, I found a small crucifix he had taken from a dead German soldier, and a battered cigarette case on which is inscribed: "5th Canadian Divisional Team Gymkhana, June 1917, Witley, England, Best Clown won by SQMS Nicol W2807." Pop also clowned his way through the Battle of the Somme, Ypres and the heavy shelling that traumatized him so thoroughly that later a thunderstorm would drive him into our basement, none of the jester to be seen.

Okay, so it's a gene thing. Pop the Clown, on active service with Mom (right). *Witley, England, 1917.*

Not often in drama does the Fool get to marry the Princess, but between the giggles and the barons of beef my patrician mater succumbed to the Best Clown, and they were married and moved into Clematis Cottage in Witley Village, a cozy, rose-swathed domicile that my mother was to remember, longingly, for years after the couple moved to more frigid quarters in Canada.

For the paternal perspective on my prenatal role in that transplantation, I quote from my father's notes on events after the Armistice. "Amelia was pregnant, and I had the choice of staying in England until Eric was born, or taking a chance and try to make Canada before the birth."

My nationality hung in the balance. One or two early contractions and I would have been born an Englishman. An exciting period of my life.

Millie and Billie chanced it. They caught the boat. Besides me (in the womb) they were worried about a beautiful Persian kitten donated by Sergeant Nicol's CO. The rough crossing gave them concern about the cat: "On board we turned it over to the galley crew which is usual with animals but our luck ran out. One day the head man told us the kitten had died. This was a great shock."

No word about how *I* took the voyage. But I think I know what was the lasting effect of being sloshed about in amniotic fluid. I hold it responsible for my acute susceptibility to motion sickness. Decades later, after I boarded the *Queen Elizabeth I* in New York City, I became violently ill. This would not have been so significant but for the fact that the ship had not yet left the dock. It was a clear case of déjà vu, my assuming the fetal position in my bunk, and hearing the ghostly meow of a feline, for the six days of the crossing to Cherbourg.

Between those two transatlantic voyages I played every variation on the theme of *mal de mer*, turning puce shade in automobiles, airplanes and elevators, on merry-go-round and ferry, even in the Cinemax. For years I felt queasy if someone even mentioned a plunging neckline.

So my progenitors arrived in Canada with a sea-green fetus, completing the discomfort of a young woman who, like thousands of other British war brides consequent to Canada's involvement in Europe's rumbles, had been blandished with accounts of this promised land of milk and honey, only to discover on landing that the milk was frozen in the bottle and the honey contested by very large bears. My mother was greeted by the middle of an Ontario winter.

My father's account of our straitened circumstances: "On arriving in Canada in Dec. we proceeded to Toronto where I [had] enlisted and received my discharge, and a grateful Canada gave me a cheque for a new suit.... Having a wife and child on the way, circumstances seemed strange and almost hopeless. No job no money."

The penniless vet with the gravid wife managed to get a job as a bookkeeping teacher in a vocational school in Kingston, Ontario. The pay was skeletal: "We found lodging—one room—in a house with a woman and some children. It was so cold there was a coat of frost on the wall paper. We were just in time for Eric was born on Dec. 28 1918 [*sic*, the year was 1919, and I have the birth certificate to prove it] without the aid of a doctor—he came later."

Then who, I wonder, *did* deliver me—Canada Post? Whoever, it is clear that I was born in cold storage, rather than in a hospital, attended by someone never identified, probably wearing mitts.

I have examined my navel for evidence that the umbilical cord was bitten off. It looks normal to me. Since the whole impromptu performance was never discussed with me, I assume that the doctor who "came later" was just able to do the cleanup job, because (a) his buggy got bogged down in a snowdrift, or (b) he was summoned because my mother developed postnatal complications, such as ice forming on the whelp.

My parents knew I was a boy because I was blue.

Needless to say, I was not circumcised. My father was too frugal a person to throw anything away that served as a wrapper.

Nor does any record exist to indicate that I was ever baptized. Maybe it was because I was born hard on Christmas and all the churches were booked. Or the fonts were frozen. In any event, despite spring thaw, I was never formally admitted to the Christian church. I have remained an unrecovered pagan. No one has ever pressured me to correct this oversight, and it is now too late, I feel, to get dunked in the blessed puddle. St. Peter, as heaven's maître d', is doubtless accustomed to that last-minute scam, tried by people who failed to make a reservation.

I hold no grudge against my parents for denying me salvation. You win some, and you lose some. Besides, they

Born with a full head of scalp. Kingston, Ontario, 1920.

must have been very busy packing: "It was necessary to find better quarters, so we rented a furnished house near the school." Where the freeze-up caused the hot-water tank to explode, along with my mother.

My father—whose autobiography breaks off abruptly at this point, since he was taken to hospital and never saw his typewriter again—gave up the job, and Ontario, for the parlous journey to find work, or at least less frost, in the more moderate clime of Vancouver, British Columbia.

I was not yet a year old and already had crossed the Atlantic, in utero, and traversed Canada, in CPR coach. This may help to explain why, today, it takes a major earthquake to get me out of the house.

Chapter 3

The Lullaby of Kingsway

There is no record of what my father called me at birth, but my mother named me "Eric," after an old boyfriend of hers in England. I learned later that he used to take her punting on the Thames. So, from Day One, my father (whose name was Bill) regarded me as a surrogate rival for my mother's affection, especially if I was holding a long pole. He never took me fishing. And that may have saved my life.

Still, I grew up hating my name and narrow, flat-bottomed boats. When forced to address me at all, my father called me "Pat," my middle name being Patrick, after my maternal grandfather. I never met him. My grandfather, that is, not my father. I met my father several times because I lived in his house for about thirty years altogether. Having only one bathroom made our meeting sort of inevitable.

My mother called me "Mannie"—a diminutive of "Little Man"—which became increasingly embarrassing after I started shaving. For years I envied Spot, our dog, because everyone called him "Spot" regardless of whether he came.

At school my surname got worked over—"Nicol Pickle"— by classmates. Having a name rhyming with a five-cent coin has dogged me into what I call adulthood, editors insisting on titling my work "Your Nicol's Worth," as if I didn't already have a criminal record for punning. How lucky some people are to be named Dollarton, or Buckley, or that honey, Money!

I wonder if any medical research has been done on the effects of one's name on self-esteem, sexual orientation, longevity and choice of beverage. If not, I am available for study as a case of terminal appellation.

My father's career as an educator ended when the Ontario government set up a commission of inquiry into why the veterans' training program wasn't working. The two events may have been connected, and led to the arrival in 1921 of fifteen cents' worth of Nicols in Vancouver, British Columbia.

My father rented a cottage in an abandoned apple orchard on Kingsway, the main thoroughfare between Vancouver and New Westminster, today glutted with used-car lots, pizza parlours and drive-in mortuaries. He used his dubious credentials to get a job with the Forest Branch of the provincial government. The only trees that concerned me, however, were the Gravensteins under whose branches I wheeled my sturdy wooden tricycle. Apple blossom is my earliest olfactory memory, a delicate scent that still brings tears to my eyes—a real menace when I'm driving in the Okanagan.

My parents made friends with another émigré English couple, known to me as "Mabel 'n Ernie." It was Ernie who liked to toss me up in the air and, if the wind was favourable, catch me before I hit the ground. Moppets are supposed to shriek with delight in response to this projection into motorless flight, but it merely reminded me of being pitched about in the womb by an overly boisterous Atlantic. Worse, on my descent from one of Ernie's launchings, my chubby leg was impaled on the sharp lead pencil he carried in his breast pocket. No one else noticed that a length of lead was embedded below my knee, and my howl of protest was attributed to my being a poor sport. When, months later, my mother did note the blue mineral deposit in my shin, there was no question of my being taken to a doctor for its extraction. Doctors were expensive in those premedicare days, and unless my entire leg turned into a Venus HB, I could expect the lead to be accepted as a weight supplement.

The pencil lead is still there in my right leg, and I shall undoubtedly be cremated with a plumbous flash in the flame. But I prefer to imagine that, thanks to Ernie, I was vaccinated early with the means to write. Other hacks have claimed to have printer's ink in their veins, but how many can pull up their pant leg to prove that they have been injected with graphite?

My mother could be excused for neglecting my writing leg. She was kept busy tending to the upper end. "Chesty," she described my condition, meaning that my bronchials were a public playground for cold germs that threatened an early quietus of my career as an author. My mother's antibiotic of choice: the mustard plaster. She tried to assuage the sheer hell of this remedy by reading to me from the first books that I remember whenever I see someone slathering his hot dog with the yellow horror.

The books were the Burgess Bedtime Stories. Listening to the travails of Poor Mrs. Quack helped to take my mind off having my tits kippered. I deeply envied Peter Rabbit for his snug refuge in the Ol' Briar Patch, safe from having his head tented over a steaming kettle until his nose was cooked. Each Burgess Bedtime Story was a slender volume, and it has occurred to me since that my father hesitated to buy a larger children's book, such as *The Wind in the Willows*, lest my wind packed it in before Mr. Toad's did.

My wheezy air-conditioning did not affect my preschooling, since none was available. I had no playmates my own age, except our large collie. Such human company as was vouchsafed me was exclusively adult, a surefire way of giving a child delusions of furniture. My parents being avid participants in the whist tournaments that were the rage of that era, I spent much of my time crawling through the forest of legs under card tables. There I gained some insights that I did not fully understand, but mostly I just annoyed the players, some of whom seemed to suspect that my parents were using me as a tactical weapon.

My chief companion was the collie, a beautiful animal, the spit and image of the Lassie that would one day bark up a storm in films. Our collie had all the looks and adventurous spirit of the screen Lassie, but none of the brains. He repeatedly ran off on crucial missions and got lost. People would bring him back to us, but except for his satisfied smile we had no idea how many children he had rescued from burning buildings, or thieves he had thwarted, or even if he had avoided knocking a blind man's cane from under him.

One day our Lassie took off and never came back. I was desolated. To be forsaken by my best friend implied that my personal charm was too scant to compensate for the absence of a fence. I became a ruminant in the orchard, drawing the long, sweet grass from its sheath to suck the soft end. I started a lifelong affair with bugs and butterflies, learning to converse with birds— chickadees, jays, and towhees—and laying the basis for a painfully shy nature, ill at ease with bipeds that don't lay eggs.

Two grins, one summer. The Kingsway, Vancouver, orchard cottage, c. 1925.

Mine being a semi-urban environment, I was deprived of the barnyard where I would at least observe the mechanics of vertebrate reproduction. If, on Kingsway, a Dodge mounted another vehicle, it was an accident. All the cars had horns, making it impossible to tell a male Ford from a female. Even if I looked underneath. Which I didn't. My father couldn't afford transportation other than the streetcar. I sometimes saw streetcars mating, but these were the interurbans, a breed that everyone knew to be pretty wild, rocketing out to the racetracks on Lulu Island. A high-stepper, the interurban was, with slippery rattan bench seats and bars on the left-side windows to prevent a kid from sticking his head out to admire another tram approaching at the combined speed of 120 miles per hour.

As sex education, however, public transit afforded me nothing of value until a decade later, when I found that one way to get next to a girl was to stand on the crowded rear platform of the tram and let an abrupt start project her into a brief intimacy, one that once brought my heel down hard on the backup bell, and got a good laugh.

The apple-orchard phase of my life ended when I was five, the Forest Branch transferring my father to Nelson, British Columbia, where he could be closer to the trees for which he was accounting. In the province's Interior, Nelson marks the appendix of a long stretch of gut called Kootenay Lake. The streets are strung up the sides of enveloping mountains so that "going downtown" can be involuntary. Seasoned residents of Nelson never walk at right angles to the pavement. Either they are sloped backward to 120 degrees to counteract the pull of gravity, or going uphill they incline sharply forward at forty-five degrees to put their noses in proximity to the sidewalk. In the 1920s kids would go downtown to the main street just for the thrill of standing upright.

Nelson is the joy of auto-brake shops. Our family didn't give them much business, because we were carless. Our house was on the same vertical avenue that gave the near-by fire hall such a fast start. The fire engine got a lot of respect in Nelson because everyone knew there was no way it was going to stop until it got to the fire, if then.

When the snows came—as they did in abundance—the perpendicularity of Nelson's streets became a sledder's paradise. One of the broader residential streets, including the intersections, was closed off to other traffic during the early hours of every winter's evening, and virtually every able-bodied child and adult in the town took to the hill. Sleighs, toboggans, bobsleds—all joined the blocks-long file trudging up one side of the course, while down the other hurtled and rattled the steel runners at speeds that would make today's snowmobiler blanch. Some of the eight-person bobsleds attained fifty miles per hour, and since there was no one left at home to baby-sit, my parents squeezed me into the crew at age six. No wonder I am now somewhat contemptuous of Winter Olympics competition. They wear helmets, the sissies.

"Track!" That yell was the only warning of our icy descent headlong through the dusk. At the bottom of the hill a crossing street presented a bump, an added hazard to life and limb. On one occasion I looked back to see my father performing a complete backward flip into our sled's wake. The impromptu somersault would have crippled a man less well cushioned by gluteus maximus.

In terms of alpine sports, Nelson of that period was not in the same class as St. Moritz, but it proved that the family that sleighed together stayed together—at least until the sled hit the bump.

The spectator winter sport to which my parents quickly became addicted was ice hockey. They became fans of the Nelson team of the Interior hockey league, following the club on the road (the railroad) for games against the hated teams of Trail and Rossland. The only way I can explain their fervour for these crazed overnight sorties is that the hockey games fed a nostalgia for World War I. The contests really had no need of a puck.

There was enough blood on the ice to keep the Red Cross going for months. Returning from the carnage, I learned to sleep in a rowdy coach of the Kettle Valley line, amid drunken singsongs, intramural brawls and strange men trying to put the hit on my mother.

Now, I think perhaps my parents were unwittingly following

the dictum of Socrates in *The Republic*, where he says that children should be taken by their elders to watch the battles of war: "Their parents may be supposed not to be blind to the risks of war, but to know, as far as human foresight can, what expeditions are safe and what dangerous." My parents blew that last bit.

Despite the distraction of the winter blood sports, however, my mother found Nelson somewhat tedious. The small-town pettiness—"Everyone knows everyone else's business"—got on her nerves. Not having any business, I was fairly enjoying the place. I was getting into my parents' musical act as a drummer. With pots pinched from our kitchen cupboard, and set up on the floor of my bedroom, and with a couple of pieces of kindling for drumsticks, I became something of a percussive prodigy, an intimation of how the Nativity's Little Drummer Boy might have sounded if summoned to Hell.

But I was good. Damn good. In no time at all I had moved my performances out of my bedroom and into the parlour, to be accompanied by mother at the piano in concerti for double boiler and frying pan. Since the tone of my tympanum could be affected by a residue of mashed potatoes, my father forked out for a real snare drum, an actual skinhead. Established as a pro, I and my mother gave a performance at a Rotary Club musicale, my taradiddle bringing down the house. The applause may have been prolonged because my mother, taking her bows, was wearing one of her shorter flapper skirts. But I found the clamour of "Encore! Encore!" intoxicating. I had to be dragged from the stage.

My musical career peaked that evening, and I never again attained the heights. What is cute at six years of age becomes a pain at seven, and grounds for homicide at eight. I turned my digital dexterity to playing marbles, the pastime that led to the first major ignominy of my life.

I let my lust to capture aggies (agates) and steelies (ball bearings) dominate my waking hours. Shooting my marble, I felt something of the power implied by the Big Bang theory of the creation of the universe. God, too, was playing marbles. And when I drew a circle on the ground with a stick, and projected my aggie at Fred's steelie, I was the prototype of the particle accelerator, scattering entities of matter at random. I proved the elegant theory that Creation was really a child's game, played with small balls of eternity.

Braced for the ship's whistle. Child abuse, aka the company picnic, c. 1926.

Unfortunately, in the heat of assimilating the galaxies of my opponent, I lost all sense of time and place. The nemesis: in hilly Nelson one of the few flat places suitable for marbles was the schoolyard of Central Elementary, where I was enrolled in Grade 1. Our class had been told to go straight home after school—a niggling prohibition for two boys huddled over the charmed circle and shooting to kill.

Thus engrossed, we were both startled by hoarse shouts emanating from the front door of the school. We looked up to see the principal, whom I'll call Mr. Torquemada (a name chosen at random). He was followed by a female teacher, both hollering and making shooing motions. With the adrenaline already pumping, my opponent and I resented this intrusion, and only after sorting out our marbles with due process did we move off, an inventory that further enraged Mr. Torquemada, who backed into the school brandishing a fist in what I took to be a gesture of authority gone bonkers.

The next morning I learned otherwise. My fellow marbles junkie and I were called into the principal's office. After dressing us down verbally for polluting the school ground with our presence after hours, Mr. Torquemada lovingly took the Strap from his desk drawer. In that time the Strap was the school counsellor. It was something even the youngest schoolchild had heard of, and was in the same category of indescribable horrors as the Bogeyman and the Dentist, only worse. Any child who "got the Strap" was seen as a write-off, morally if not physically. And here I was, looking at this medieval instrument of punishment, as Mr. Torquemada smacked it with anticipation against his leg.

The Strap was a broad length of black leather at least a quarter inch thick. Where school principals got their straps in those days, or even today, I have no idea. Maybe there was a school supplies company called Captain Bligh Specialties, which also provided the blackboard chalk that sent shivers up my spine.

The other kid got it first, with me standing and watching. I have never, or hardly ever, come first in any event. Getting the Strap was just another of those contact sports where there was a clear disadvantage in being the runner-up, with ample time to watch the preview of my own ordeal.

The other kid howled before the whip even hit his outstretched palm. He was smart, that lad. He put on a satisfying display of vociferous suffering that got him off with only a couple of wallops. He left, sobbing, as Mr. Torquemada turned his attention to me.

"Left hand, please," he said, smiling, much as Satan may have smiled coiled in that earlier Tree of Knowledge.

I refused to cry. The Strap blistered my palm again and again, but like a damn fool I just stood there feeling my face go as red as my shocked fingers. Peeved, breathing hard—perhaps a bit out of condition for this workout—Mr. Torquemada flailed away with added vehemence. I had to wonder how I would adapt to life with a stumped wrist, like Captain Hook. I might never play the drums again.

"Get out!" the principal ordered, panting as he tossed the Strap back into his drawer. "Go back to your class."

This I did, wordlessly, entering the classroom and flinching at all the eyes swivelled to look at the renegade who had paid the supreme penalty. I sat at my desk, and for the first time looked at my left hand. It was grotesquely purple and swollen, a veritable catcher's mitt. The hand of shame. I hated every throbbing crease of it—the life line, the love line, the lot. What was writ there in scarlet script was "Disgrace." Yet I couldn't squeeze out a tear.

I never told my parents about my day of infamy. The hand subsided quickly, but the psychological effect of the episode has endured. I have remained incapable of crying about anything. I missed my chance to be attractive to today's woman as a guy sensitive enough to weep. I blame the educational system for creating a rebel rendered stoic. A kid with an attitude. One that would get me into trouble all my life.

Today, if a school principal tenderized my left hand with the Strap, he might be sued by the coach of my Little League baseball team, because I was a southpaw. I write with my right, but throw and bat left-handed. The cerebral hemispheres that are supposed to define which-handedness have obviously refused to accept responsibility in my case, hoping that my feet will make up my mind. This ambivalence was respected by Mr. Squeers of Dotheboys Hall: he birched a boy on his bottom. Whether right-cheeked or left-cheeked, the boy would not have his grip on the cricket bat impaired by the flogging. Canadian educators still had much to learn, circa 1926.

My father spanked me only once. About this time I accompanied my mother to the five-and-dime store whose toy department glittered for me as the ultimate bazaar of earthly delights, none of which my mother was prepared to buy for me. Cruising at nose level past a display of midget model cars, I saw a gold roadster with spoke wheels that totalled my control of my hand. The hand, living a life of its own, reached out, seized the prize and put it into my pocket. A lightning strike. Later, at home, I was playing with this beauty on the floor when my mother discovered us, and how I came by this possession.

"Your father will deal with you," she told me.

I would have preferred that my mother dealt with me, or that God dealt with me, or that almost anyone not built as burly as my father dealt with me. I spent two miserable hours cowering behind the sofa before Retribution came home and...I guess, spanked me. I don't remember that part. I know that he didn't take me out to the woodshed. We didn't own a woodshed. But I can see now how the threat of the woodshed helped to discipline my generation of kids, a correctional facility since lost to central heating.

My self-esteem being entirely dependent on my parents, I strove hard to make amends at school. The same year that I got the strap, I was awarded a diploma—for Deportment. I showed diligence in becoming the teacher's pet. Female teachers seemed to like me, so this primary-grade sycophant copped a whole series of diplomas, which schools then were smart enough to award for almost any activity, including showing up (Attendance).

Besides making out with the female teachers, I hit it off with little girls after school. The little girl next door, Billie Wallace, was very knowlegeable about indoor games played in the basement of her house, notably one called Doctor. Never having been to a doctor, I had to be instructed in the rules of the game by Billie and a couple of other dedicated female physicians, who had no difficulty in convincing me that a thorough medical examination was essential to determine my problem, regardless of whether I had one. The patient readily dropped his shorts, and was lying prone on the operating bench, enjoying the diagnostic skill of Billie's hands assessing his bare bum, when the ER was consternated by the sound of unmistakably adult feet descending the basement stairs. A miracle recovery! The patient was back on his feet and running, impaired only by frantically hoisting his knickers.

Mercifully Billie's mother never billed my family for medical treatment. Since it occurred decades before pediatricians like Spock and Gesell reassured parents that sex play is perfectly normal among young children, I lucked out. Still, the trauma of being caught in flagrante delicto, debagged and debased, not only left me with a lifelong dread of medical examinations but also affected my relations with young women for some time—almost a year, actually. Not until I was eight or so did I recover my trust in games that girls liked to play: Spin the Bottle, Postman's Knock, Forfeits, all of which involved kissing and giggling in quantity.

This, however, was to be the halcyon period of my womanizing. Between nine and nineteen I retreated into a shell of shyness that abstracted me totally from the company of girls. When girls developed those enigmatic bumps under their blouses, they became for me a dangerous mystery, terribly alluring, but imbued with some ineffable Life Force that I felt incompetent to deal with.

Because neither of my parents attended church, I received no formal religious instruction. As a kid, I thought that all angels were named Harold—the Harold Angels—who had to be harked regularly.

These angels were named after God, whose name was also Harold. The Lord's Prayer—which I picked up from ululations before class in elementary school—addressed "Our Father, who's Art in Heaven, Harold be thy name." I never figured out why God was Art in Heaven. Maybe he needed

Fifteen cents' worth of Nicols, holidaying on Salt Spring Island, British Columbia, c. 1932.

two names because He travelled a lot.

The Harold people were not to be confused with the Ark angels, who helped Noah build his houseboat, which was no big deal. Being raised in Vancouver, I was not particularly impressed by the story of the Flood, because its raining for forty days and forty nights was fairly normal precipitation to a West Coaster.

I once saw a photo of the Holy Land in a Bible that an English relative had sent me in vain hope of rescuing a heathen, and I concluded that it was a very dry place that could use a good Vancouver deluge. Noah must have just panicked.

Chapter 4

Our Ship Comes in a Scow

Besides my mother's ennui in the small town, a factor in our leaving Nelson after only a few years may have been my father's aversion to the thunderstorms that rumbled around the mountains like the Lord's bowling alley. His overseas units had been shelled so fiercely in France that he was spooked by any sound resembling those explosions, and he would take shelter in the basement until the bad vibes diminished. Vancouver was not only relatively free of electrical storms but also large enough to diffuse the shock waves when my mother danced the Charleston. We moved back to the coast city's East Side in time for me to enter Grade 2. The Nelson school apparently did not forward my criminal record as a trespass artist, since I was admitted to the school without a body search for concealed marbles.

My father had been felled by the Forest Branch, or else had proved deciduous, as he entered one of his brief entrepreneurial phases, partnering with another man in an auto-painting business. What made him think that he could make his fortune spraying paint on cars, I can't guess. It may have been an outbreak of his love/hate relationship with automobiles, an affair begun in Oshawa when he worked for McLaughlin-Buick. I know that once he acquired an auto of his own, I was into a sibling-rivalry situation where I had the short end of his affection. I was a mama's boy and a daddy's bane because I threw up on his back seat.

His auto-paint business soon went belly-up, but even today, when I enter a body shop to retrieve the car whose dink has been doctored, the smell of vaporized paint carries me back sixty years to the way my father smelled when he came home from work. Added to the ambient smoke produced by parents who were both tobacco addicts, these leaded fumes doubtless fuelled the rhinitis that made me a ten-hankies-a-day boy for years.

Surrendering his spray gun, my father retreated once more into the dull but lead-free job of accounting. This time his employer was a Howe Street brokerage firm, and since the Crash of '29 was still misted by rosy futures, the company prospered. Our family fortunes took a sharp upturn, and we moved from the East Side to the West Side into a bungalow hard by the Endowment Lands of the University of British Columbia. My father bought the house outright for $1,250. Still very much alive, the property today is worth at least $400,000.

This part of Vancouver (Point Grey) had only recently become part of the city, graduating from being a bushy municipality that prided itself on its well water and cultural closeness to the province's only university. Better yet, our house was only a block from both the area's elementary school (Langara) and the city's most prestigious high school (Lord Byng). Thus, for most of my schooling I enjoyed the advantage that counts most for a well-adjusted student: I could come home for lunch.

Indeed, my coming home for the midday meal became such a vital part of my formal education that when I entered UBC I biked the three miles home to scoff up the scrambled eggs or baked beans on toast. My poor mother never got a break from my inexorable pillaging of her noon hour. Day after day, year after year, there I was, salivating, a hard-working student who gave her no excuse to get a life of her own.

Today, of course, I would never get away with such demand on her time. I would be hanging around the school, eating my peanut-butter sandwich and submitting to the peer pressures to discover all those exciting possibilities for mischief that require our schools to be patrolled by police-men.

My mother did, however, have some advantages denied to the modern mom. She never had to go shopping for food at the supermarket. There *was* no supermarket. Instead, all the food came to *her*. Fruit and veggies were conveyed per-sonally to her back door by the Chinese farmer of same. If she wished to inspect the produce, she merely had to walk to the lane where Mr. Low Fat's Model T truck spread its tailboard panoply of lettuce, carrots, apples and other fruits of the fertile Fraser Valley, so fresh that the cutworms in the cabbage had not yet realized that they were now living in a mobile home.

Those carrots tasted like carrots, not like the moot roots incarcerated in a cello bag at the supermarket. Nor did the strawberries come from California, with all that this meant in getting less blah for the buck. Certain produce my mother could buy only in season, but I never missed having broccoli year-round. I was strong on milk, butter and eggs, alone or in combination, all of which the Lower Mainland supplied in abundance.

The daily deliveries of almost everything—milk, hen-fresh eggs, bread and patisserie, Douglas teas and Turkish Delights (borne in the rattrap of Mr. Douglas's stout Raleigh one-speed)—assured that my mother was never lonely. Only a brass band was needed to complete the parade of trades-men to our front and back doors. My mother had more male company during a week than most women today enjoy unless they set up housekeeping under a lamppost.

For us kids the regular delivery of ice for the icebox was a uniquely festive occasion. On a hot summer's day the ice wagon had a wake of small humans who watched the ice-man chip off each block, savagely seize it with his tongs, sling it over his leathered shoulder and disappear into a house long enough for us to snatch up the mouth-chilling shards and suck from them such cool satisfaction as is taken for granted by the Pepsi Generation.

Most of these vehicles being horse-drawn, we often gained the bonus of steaming balls of fertilizer for the gar-den's roses. It was horse-apple roulette in the lane. Behind whose house would the nag drop her bounty? When it was our house that got lucky, I was quick to pick up the perks in a box. Not a blue box, but still a racy kind of recycling.

And, finally, our preeminent visitor—the postie. Not a lit-ter carrier but a mailman, who came twice a day, six days a week, usually with actual mail, i.e., letters written by hand, from people who were not merely trying to make a mass-mailing offer look as personal as a massage. Our postie was someone more than a stranger in blue shorts jamming tracts into our mail slot. He was the same guy, year after year. We were family. We cared about him, he cared about us, and our Boxing Day present to him betokened a meaningful relationship. Try to get *that* on-line, Internet.

The only provision for which my mother needed to leave the comfort of her own home was meat. Her meat order would, of course, be delivered later by the butcher's boy on his bike, but she liked to keep our butcher on his toes by making a personal appearance a couple of times a week to examine his joints and tweak his chops. If she found a bone chip in our cleavered ribs, Mr. Beatty heard about it, and when I discovered a long, fat worm in my portion of baked halibut, what he got from my mother was the verbal equivalent of being hung up on one of his own meat hooks.

Today, when I do the shopping at the supermarket, I am humbly grateful if I can even get the attention of one of the meat cutters in their glass sanctuary. And if I treated him or her the way my mother dealt with Mr. Beatty, the meat cutters' union would have my guts for ground beef on special.

Perhaps my childhood was the poorer, my being denied the experience of riding perched in a baskart propelled up and down aisles of goodies that I was told not to touch. But I suspect that my taste buds have been degraded by the megamart that sells both turkeys and rubber beach balls, processed cheese and plastic placemats, bread and sponges. There must be a more savoury way to meet a checkout girl.

Because our house in Point Grey was only a block from the University Endowment Lands—several hundred acres of urban wilderness that was the natural habitat of raccoons, coyotes, rabbits, a heronry and smaller prey for a boy who fancied himself as a character out of the Old Wild West—I spent much of my leisure time loping along the trails with other Hopalong Cassidys. My mother never seemed to worry about my playing Cowboys and Indians in this forest where, even today, it is easy for a person to get lost. Despite the rumours about a nude hermit living in the denser part of the UEL, the danger of molestation of their children did not pre-occupy parents as much in that time. I think that, if any-thing, had a pedophile made a move on me, my parents' sympathy would have been for the creep. Reason: I would have shot him with my .45.

My .45 was not the adult model, but a weapon of similar calibre fashioned from eight inches of beanpole (the barrel) with a wooden butt to which was nailed a clothes-peg (the trigger). The ammo was a strip of rubber inner tube stretched from the muzzle to the trigger, which merely had to be squeezed to release the rubber with enough force to demolish a naked attacker's libido. My aim was deadly. I could splat a fly on the wall from twenty feet. As for anyone trying to seduce me with candy or sweet talk, no way. In those days adults spoke to a child mainly to distance them-selves from a nuisance. Had anyone tried to touch me, any-where but in a shoe store trying to fit me with runners, I would have gunned him down.

My infatuation with guns—any kind of gun smaller than that found on HMS *Hood*—was total in these preteen years. When I was about ten, my parents gave me a Daisy air rifle for Christmas, a weapon that greatly increased my firepower. There were then no fussy regulations about discharging pellet guns inside city limits, so that it was quite natural for me to engage in a shooting war with Stewart De Vitt, who lived in the house opposite ours across Sixteenth Avenue. I had nothing in particular against Stewart, but since he was the only other kid in the block who owned an air rifle, he automatically became Kaiser Wilhelm, Chief Sitting Bull and

Al Capone all rolled into one target.

The climactic battle raged for almost an hour, with me firing from behind the embankment of our front lawn and Stewart bobbing up from his front porch rail for potshots, with brief truces while vehicles or pedestrians traversed no-man's-land. It ended when one of my pellets hit Stewart above the eye, and he had to retire from the front. His parents later complained mildly to mine, who in turn asked me to avoid shooting any more De Vitts.

But no attempt was made to curtail my zest for firearms. On the contrary, for my twelfth birthday my parents gave me a .22 single-shot sports rifle, and with it the capability to terrorize any form of life up to a quarter mile away (farther, when shooting across water). Only once did I have my .22 temporarily confiscated, by a Mountie who spotted me picking off crows on the public beach of Ganges, Saltspring Island, in the Strait of Georgia, where our family was holidaying. Even though my beloved ordnance was returned to me when we left the island, I was miffed at the implication that my shooting was a menace to life higher up the food chain, such as tourists. Not only was I a damn good shot, but I scrupulously restricted my live targets to crows and rats, both black-hearted thieves that deserved to ingest a Whiz-Bang short.

The guns were the only educational toys I got, except for one Meccano set that I fashioned into spindly pistols and fondled at the Alma Cinema during a Saturday matinee showing of Tom Mix decimating the aboriginal population of North America. Yet, by the time I was old enough to go to war for real (World War II), my passion for firearms was utterly spent. Ballistically speaking, I was a burnout. I scored well on the firing range, but the thrill just wasn't there. I turned down the opportunity to be a tail gunner in an RCAF bomber because it was somehow *vieux chapeau*.

Today I abhor hunting and am terrified of firearms. Is there perhaps a lesson here to be noted by experts in child behavioural psychology? Does my history of precocious, juvenile lust for violence suggest that, instead of giving little boys dolls to play with, with a view to gentling the spirit and producing peace-loving adults, parents should be giving little girls models of the Uzi automatic rifle? This would enable both sexes to get bloody-mindedness out of their systems before people were old enough either to join feminist organizations or go murdering the inoffensive moose. Just a thought.

Chapter 5

The Perils of Puberty

One place where my parents did not allow me a free range with my .22 was Stanley Park. The park was too crowded, even in the 1930s, to permit unlicensed fusillades at fauna. So I sat glumly in the back seat of the green Essex sedan that my father had bought as *his* offensive weapon, and which every Sunday he wheeled around the park as a ritual in lieu of our going to church.

For Vancouverites, then as now, the circumnavigation of Stanley Park was one of the solemn rites of the Sabbath. It was as though the Almighty were an ecologist to be appeased by this pilgrimage around the park's natural wilderness. We were a slow procession of vehicles that began at Lost Lagoon, bowed to Brockton Point, made obeisance to the pine-capped prelate that was Siwash Rock, then continued on to the votive teahouses and bowling greens to conclude at English Bay. Once there, my father angle-parked the Essex at the promenade so we could watch the ambulant beach-worshippers who had emerged from Kitsilano Gothic mansions and the stylite flats of the West End.

God, how I hated Sundays! And other legal holidays. Encapsulation in the Essex was impossible to avoid, my father being tireless in his determination to explore every desolate strand, every vertiginous mountain summit, that the car could be bullied to attain. The hood ornament on the Essex was, in fact, a real thermometer, so that my father could watch the red column climb without taking his eyes off the hot, dusty road. He had a florid complexion that grew rapidly redder, and a military moustache that bristled at the challenge of reaching the top of the simmering hill before the radiator cap blew off. Instead of a tape deck my mother and I had Pop's expletives, addressed to the hypersensitive hood ornament.

In winter the gauge reversed, and my father cursed the confirmation that the cooling system was frozen solid. A tea kettle was standard equipment on our motor outings. Depending on the season, I was designated to fill the kettle either with cold water from the nearest creek or hot water from the nearest dwelling. I also had to act as flagman while my father changed a flat tire, another regular feature of our fun trips, which afforded him ample opportunity to comment on the family background of the Essex manufacturer, car salesmen, and the highways department responsible for the washboard road.

My mother endured these outbursts with a pained silence that merely aggravated my father's fury. He knew that her withdrawal was a criticism of his own family background.

Nor did I help matters by welcoming every unscheduled stop as an opportunity to throw up. Often Pop had to pull over to the side of the road when there was nothing wrong with the car so that I could retch freely. This disgusted him, proving that I had a problem not covered by warranty.

Double jeopardy for me was our automotive trips to Blaine, Washington, so that my parents could smuggle back cartons of American cigarettes, particularly prized as being more narcotic than Canadian brands. In this caper it was my job to sit on the contraband, which was under a car rug, and look innocent when the customs officer asked us, "Anything to declare?" I shook my head in unison with my role models, but always feared that the officer would scent my having wet my pants.

This early introduction to bald-faced lying by my parents had the effect of convincing me that I would never make it as a Baron Munchausen. It forced me into a life of telling the truth. This may explain some of my subsequent social isolation, as well as my never having been asked to run for public office. Not only was I kiln-dried by secondhand smoke, but my potential as a prevaricator was stunted. I would never write a book entitled *The Joy of Fibbing*.

However, smuggling US coffin nails *en famille* didn't put me off my own private criminal pursuit: scoffing golf balls. Part of the University Endowment Lands was occupied by the University Golf Club, whose rough included small, murky ponds in which darted polliwogs and salamanders— legitimate prey for small boys whose ulterior motive was to find lost golf balls, preferably before they stopped bouncing. A parlous poaching, this, as the golf club employed rangers—big, rough fellows carrying clubs not approved by St. Andrews and usually accompanied by an equally vicious dog with which to chase off raiders of the lost hook. My transition from ball hunting to pond peering had to be extremely nimble as the brutes thundered past in pursuit of larger intruders.

But the risk of a whack on the head was worth it for me, since finding golf balls became one of the major addictions of my preteen years. I became knowledgeable about the cunning ways in which a golf ball will hide. (I once found a beautifully dimpled Dunlop in the crotch of a cottonwood tree.) I learned that the repaints were easiest to find, being too old and too disfigured to choose their refuge with care. But a brand-new, driven-only-once-by-a-wealthy-widow ball, ah, that was a thrill to pluck from its leafy lair. A junkie's buzz, it was. The quasi-sensual sensation of unearthing buried treasure.

Some of the golf balls I found I sold to other collectors, such as my father. But the most prized—like the vintage stamp or wine—I kept in a temperature-controlled closet, occasionally pouring them over my head with Volponish cackles as though confident that one day gold, as the world's precious commodity of exchange, would be replaced by the golf ball. In fact, I was so busy being a miser of balls that I didn't notice that my own had dropped. I have no recollection of finding anything significant in my pubic rough. But I shall never forget the clump of crabgrass that concealed the ultraspecial Spalding.

But my parents were not content to leave me to my swampy ponds. Being British, a seagoing race, they seemed to feel obliged to support Britannia's rule of the waves by subjecting the three of us to a horror of that era: the Company Picnic. This annual watery safari consisted of piling the employees and their families into one of the coastal galleys of Union Steamships, which waddled up and down local inlets to deliver their human sacrifice to remote picnic grounds. Of special interest to my motion sickness was their flair for concentrating all the misery of an English Channel crossing into half the time. The skippers got their jollies from blowing the whistle the moment I took my fingers out of my ears. Their timing was impeccable, which was more than could be said for the washrooms.

I could never understand why my parents exposed us to the Company Picnic. To leave a comfortable home in Vancouver, with its handy, superb beaches and parks, and be borne in a tacky, funnelled tub to some godforsaken campsite whose cooking facility was a communal pit that would shock a Kwakiutl, with matching latrine—this baffled me then, as it does now. I know that the English take their pleasures sadly but, damn it, I'm a Canadian.

It was during a family safari to Bowen Island that I had one of those encounters that remain soldered to the memory long after all other details have vanished. As we were walking up the wharf, a teenage female wearing an adhesive sweater confronted me, thrust her perky breasts at me and said, "Take two. They're small!" Then she rejoined her friends in a gale of giggles.

This episode reinforced my belief that I was, obviously to all, a sexual simpleton. Not only did I not know all the answers, I didn't understand the questions. I failed to comprehend my own body, let alone that of the opposite sex, which could be launched at me without warning.

Having neither brother nor sister to live with, I was relatively disadvantaged in the area of comparative anatomy. This limited my research to the scrawny object that gazed back at me from the mirror, with an expression of revulsion.

Not only was I not street-smart, I was also as dumb as dirt *indoors*. I had never even heard the word *penis*. To me the thing was just It. Personal hygiene was negligible. I was afraid to wash It in case It shrank.

Back at school, Langara Elementary, I got report cards that repeatedly ranked me second in the class. Always a bridesmaid...Today I would be a straight-A student, or more likely had my ugly competitive spirit muffled in a waffling verbal appraisal. But in that era of brutal precision in the ranking of a pupil's stupidity and/or apathy, the report was not alphabet soup. To be ranked second undoubtedly looked preferable to the kid who was ranked thirtieth in a class of twenty-nine. But to me it shouted that, once again, I had failed to be Number One. At the time I didn't understand that this was a disguised blessing, in that I wasn't peaking too early, academically. I escaped being fondled by the bitch goddess, Success. I had the stimulus to keep trying, something that I shall carry to the grave—the grave that is second from the top of the hill.

On the minus side my bringing home diplomas proved to be hazardous to my health. One day my mother phoned my father at work to tell him I had bagged another honour scroll, then handed me the receiver of the wall phone. But, on returning to the kitchen, she didn't notice that my right hand was in the jamb when she slammed the door. My moment of triumph was thus punctuated by the crunch of knuckle. I had heard that God punishes pride, but surely this was overdoing it? One finger now jutted out at a strange angle, demolishing my chance of becoming a great concert pianist, unless they found me a piano with gappy keys.

My parents apparently accepted the loss to the concert stages of the world, as they did not take my dislocated finger to the doctor. These being the days before medicare, my father was a great believer in the power of the body to heal itself of anything short of decapitation. I never saw a doctor for any of my ailments: measles, chicken pox, bronchitis, ankle sprain. The result was that I grew up convinced that the only condition that would warrant my receiving medical attention would be a mortal illness—consumption, rabies, sheep rot—or some disease too shameful to be allowed into the house, say, Black Death, or some anomaly in the private parts.

Although spared leprosy, I suffered from a malady only slightly less loathsome: eczema. I knew the agony of psoriasis when it was still called mange. My revolting skin condition advertised itself on my hands and legs: patches of red, scaly, maddeningly itchy blisters that, when scratched, became running sores that not even a mother could love. My mother surmised that I had picked up mange from our dog, Spot. Spot was indeed a scrofulous mongrel, but it did nothing for my self-esteem to believe that, in addition to rather prominent canine teeth, I had a pestilence not normally associated with animals that walk on their hind legs. Half a century later I was to learn from an allergist that one of the early signs of nonallergenic vasomotor rhinitis is persistent skin rash.

During the years that mattered, however, all I knew was that I had these foul blotches on my hide, and that if I ever expected to hold hands with a girl I would have to provide her with a pair of rubber gloves.

It is my theory that the eczema was a major factor in isolating me socially, and causing the introversion that is hell on one's love life but essential to other kinds of creative activity. Just as the irritant grain of sand is what moves the oyster to make the pearl, my eczema made me clam up and keep my hands to myself and writing. Novelist John Updike, in his autobiography, cites the same problem—juvenile psoriasis—as the prime source of his living in his own head, and finding there characters to whom he didn't need to explain his prurigo.

This benefit takes time, however. For the afflicted kid the immediate prospect is that of having to walk through life ringing a bell and mumbling, "Unclean...unclean..."

Being a manifest freak, I distanced myself, literally, from my schoolmates when we were lined up each morning...to be marched to classes. I hung back, resisting both the regimentation and the dust scuffled to the detriment of my watery beezer. This got me marched once again into the office of the principal, where I got a tongue-lashing for insubordination. If anything, this hurt worse than the Strap. Injustice! Who of us ever forgets his or her first encounter with this hairy brute fact of life? We may forget the circumstances of our first kiss, or our first rectal examination, but for none does the scene dim of being put down by the unjust, by the abuse of power that mauls our faith in human nature.

It is the lesson that many once learned in school, especially the English school. Charles Dickens made the classroom tyranny the springboard for his soaring attacks on all manner of injustice, and I picked up a bit of the action at Langara when accused of lying through the nose I was trying to protect. The mutinous spirit seeded in the principal's office was to land me, in later years, in reckless conflict with Authority, such as my going AWOL from a compulsory air force church parade because I was a devout agnostic.

If revenge is, as the Sicilians say, something best eaten cold, the hatred of injustice is best engendered in school so that it can mature properly instead of making feeble pouts at payment of income tax. In my opinion one of the gravest delinquencies of today's public-school system is that the teachers and administrators are so compulsively fair and amiable that the average young person can graduate without even the basics of moral outrage. Kids must depend entirely on their parents, or their peers, to be able to identify with Hamlet's citing "the oppressor's wrong, the proud man's contumely..." A little pedagogical oppression, like a flu shot, and despite the side effect of temporary nausea, can provide lifetime immunity to conformance.

In the fall of 1933 I entered Grade 9 at Lord Byng High School. The elevation from elementary to high was not as causative of altitude sickness as it is today. For one thing, high schools were less populous then. They did not require such a giddy leap from being a big frog in a small pond to being a worm in the compost heap. Also to my advantage, Lord Byng was a prestigious school whose rotund principal, Mr. Morrow, was a no-nonsense teacher of the classics, his curriculum reflecting his strong conviction that a student unschooled in Latin had missed not merely an elective but the postulate for literacy. His star Latin teacher, Miss Lawrence, who was also the club-wielding coach of the girls' field-hockey team, was formidable enough to put the wind straight up Julius Caesar himself. She ruled over our Latin class as though determined that what happened to the Roman Empire would never befall Point Grey as long as she had the strength to deal out another homework assignment.

Fearful of being divided, like Gaul, into three parts, I went head-to-head with *hic, haec, hoc* and got riddled with the roots of most of the words you are reading. Although Miss Lawrence never let us anywhere near Ovid, let alone the raunchy graffiti of Pompeii, I put in a lot of miles with Caesar's legions, with no R and R.

Oddly my weakest subject in Grade 9 was English. Our teacher was a petite, attractive young woman whose response to a fractious student was to burst into tears. For this reason I couldn't achieve the same degree of terror in

English as in Latin. Only in later grades, with a nonlachrymose male teacher, did my writing begin to show some discipline other than not going off the edge of the paper. At no point in my English instruction was expression exalted over grammar, as appears to be the priority today. I wouldn't have known a haiku from a hiccup. Assigned the traditional essay topic "What I Did on My Summer Vacation," I would not have got extra marks for writing it in the shape of a tent.

Canadian education had not yet fallen under the influence of the uncorseted theories of Rousseau and Dewey, which today ensure the graduation of the happy savage or none at all. Spelling errors were not admired as innovative. Learning by rote was rampant, and I learned how to memorize whole sheaves of notes and reproduce them on an exam—a skill deprecated today, but my memory's data bank was not dependent on the bowel movements of a mouse.

As for sex education, mine was limited to studying the legs of the girls in the halls between classes. Fleeting instruction, at best, the glimpse of bobby-socked ankle. And quite disturbing enough. Mercifully the pleated skirts were worn long during the 1930s. Otherwise I might have done myself permanent damage by stepping on my own tongue. Anyway, I lusted at arm's length. No dates. Between the eczema and the heavy demands of homework, I was as celibate as a monk. In fact, there have been popes whose sex lives were more baroque than what I contrived in high school.

When I was about thirteen, my mother made a brave stab at dispelling my magisterial ignorance about sex. I'm sure she had hoped that I would pick up some information in the conventional manner of the time, i.e., in the gutter. But I never seemed to be in the gutter when instructive conversation entered the sewer. Also, our street didn't have a gutter. It had a ditch, which didn't get around much. And watching dogs "do it" hadn't helped, either, because few girls hung around fire hydrants.

"Fuck you!" I had heard kids offer this advice, and had beaten up a neighbour kid when he addressed the suggestion to me. But I hadn't the foggiest notion of the physiological basis for the obscenity. To tell the truth, I *still* don't understand the mechanics of "Fuck you!" Unless the receptor is double-jointed, the conjunction seems illusory.

Anyway, the question that cornered my mother into having to deal with my dimness was the traditional "Mom, where do babies come from?" From what I had been able to glimpse of female anatomy, the only possible exit for the baby was the navel. A rather small departure bay, in my view. My hypothesis was also flawed by the fact that men had navels, too, as well as tits that had no documented purpose other than to relieve the monotony of the chest.

My mother grasped at the well-chewed straw: the example of the birds and the bees. When no light went on in my eyes, she went to pencil and paper, drawing me a picture of a well-endowed bee probing a blossom that had generous hips.

At last the penny dropped. I was appalled.

"That's *disgusting*," I said.

"You'll change your mind when you get older," said my mother, making one of the major understatements of our time.

However, being slightly better informed about human reproduction had no immediate effect on my diffidence toward girls. If anything, I became even more prone to yearning from afar. I didn't chase girls because, like the dog chasing a car, I wouldn't know what to do if I caught one.

Not only did I graduate from high school without having penetrated the blossom, but I never got out of the hive. My first kiss as a teenager never happened, since I was twenty-one before the first girl I had dated, after waiting for a year, got fed up and kissed *me*. She paid for it with the worst case of beard burn seen in those parts.

Today such inhibited behaviour toward the opposite sex would be diagnosed as (a) latent homosexuality, or (b) apprenticeship as a eunuch, or (c) the only case of bad breath ever to elicit a warning from the World Health Organization. For my time, however, I was by no means a sexual oddity. The Great Depression—as it came to be called, though while living them I had no idea that the 1930s were all that dirty—was a natural vasectomy. It meant that high-schoolers did not have cars, or access to cars. We had bikes. The absence of the extra two wheels was a major factor in preserving the virginity of both sexes prior to graduation and certainly *during* graduation. The annual fertility rite of hiring a limo for a group orgy presumes a parental affluence that in the 1930s was so exceptional as to be statistically, and socially, insignificant.

Liquor was just barely legal after the Prohibition years. A kid really had to work at it to establish the excuse of being stoned at the moment of impregnation. With abortion outlawed, and no safety nets of welfare and support groups, teenage pregnancy was a fate, if not worse than death, certainly more stressful than a bad cold. If a girl got "knocked up," the boy responsible was under considerable pressure to marry her, find a job and not add to the fiscal problems of Prime Minister Mackenzie King. (The PM set us a good example as a bachelor whose only serious involvement was with his dog and his dead mother.)

Masturbation. I had never seen or heard the word until I

filled out the enlistment form to join the Royal Canadian Air Force, on which the practice was listed with venereal disease as a fatal flaw in one's capability to bugger Hitler. Nor had I read enough of the Old Testament to be aware that spilling one's seed upon the ground was not part of the federal grain program. But some instinctual taboo denied me the quick fix of onanism. I was beset by the same *diable au corps* as the lad who, being warned that abusing himself could render him blind, asked, "Is it okay if I just do it till I need glasses?"

Another medical consideration, whispered in the school washroom, was "Hair will grow on the palms of your hands." From this I divined that the thing had to be done no-hands, a skill I associated with riding a bike. Amazingly I managed this by standing on my neck and bending backward until my vertebrae played a rhapsody for xylophone.

I didn't make my sexual tension any less hard on spinal discs by reading French novels. One reason why I got good grades in French was that the local private lending library carried a modest stock of works by Guy de Maupassant, Emile Zola and lesser blue lights, with expurgated bits indicated by a row of asterisks. Having a vivid if confused imagination, I was readily turned on by asterisks, which I still regard as the sexiest punctuation mark in all of grammar. The exclamation point, or schoolgirl shriek, isn't even in it as a cheap thrill! See?

The steamy, bodice-ripping, neck-biting novels—though none of them as sexually explicit as the stuff boldly available in any supermarket today—were not something I would dare to take home. I had to read them in situ while Mrs. Ridgewell was busy attending to another customer. If she came into the stacks, I quickly stashed the throbbing romance and pulled out a harmless Charlie Chan. I didn't learn much, despite all the heaving of bosom and monsoon deluge of kisses, but it was an introduction to speed reading. Those novels got my words per minute up, among other things.

The golden age of comic books not yet having emerged from the egg, boys of my generation had to content themselves with publications whose verbal content went beyond *Splat!* or *Bam!* or *Zoom! The Boys Own Annual*, *Adventure* and the mighty, imperial, red-cover *Chums* offered stories of action and heroism with the same moral values as the later *Superman* but with a vocabulary that assumed that the reader had evolved beyond a diet of bamboo shoots. The Tom Swift series of books enchanted me because Tom enjoyed such a marvellous sequence of labour-saving machines—*Tom Swift and His Electric Rifle*, *Tom Swift and His Amazing Kite...*

He never, however, came up with the invention that I would have killed for: *Tom Swift and His Magic Sawdust Burner*. Sawdust was what we fed our furnace in our house, as did many West Coasters because of the abundance of sawdust from local sawmills. The way it, and I, worked was that most of our basement was partitioned for a huge bin into which navvies dumped sacks of sawdust each fall, while I shovelled it into young mountains without my being buried in an avalanche of coniferous rubble. Atop the furnace sat the hungry hopper that it was my job to keep fed with sawdust from the bin. Our thermostat, upstairs, consisted of a chain that, when yanked or lowered, adjusted the draft of the furnace and either slowed or accelerated the feed of the sawdust. This system combined central heating with the less desirable features of living atop Mount Vesuvius.

Because the hopper got clogged readily, the furnace, at least once a week in winter, exploded hot ash from its fiery grate into the basement. A heating inspector's worst night-mare—that was our furnace. But I was quite attuned to the eruptive *whoomf* that signalled a mad scramble downstairs to contain the smouldering debris. The furnace obviously hated us. It may have resented that I kept my pet rabbit, Smokey, in the sawdust bin. Smokey loved the bin because he could tunnel into the sawdust, but his droppings did, as the winter progressed, exacerbate the digestive problems of the furnace hopper, besides creating an aromatic ambience upstairs that caused guests to wonder if we had reverted to the aboriginal fuel of buffalo chips.

Since I was the designated tender of the clinkered inferno, my winter recreational activities were basement-oriented. Besides the sawdust bin there was just enough room for a Ping-Pong table, though this had to be folded out of the way when my chum and I picked up the foils and fenced, wear-ing my mother's soup strainers as face masks. The violent swordplay, against a background of sprayed sparks, dis-couraged my parents from venturing below the main deck. My father paid for the sawdust but preferred not to see for himself how Smokey's active bladder kept the sawdust moist, slowing combustion and saving on fuel cost. A model rabbit, Smokey was.

Thanks to the athletic facility of our cellar, I became adept enough at table tennis to cop a cup in the Vancouver junior tournament. I also won a Point Grey tennis meet. Racket games were as macho as I got. For me, no contact sports, like rugby. The prospect of having a guy's arms around my waist turned me off.

Chapter 6

Dirtied by the Thirties

I blame the frustrated-jock factor for my failing to be awarded the Nobel Prize for Literature. My writing career was blighted by the handicap of my having quick reflexes and a reasonably healthy body. Successful authors may have an early phase of indulgence in sports, but they usually shake it off before it becomes detrimental to their concentrating on their art. The Muse does not wear a jogging bra. *Au contraire*, the history of literature shows that its creators are not slaves to the adrenal gland. The consumptive Keats, the blind Milton, the stoned Coleridge— these are the prototype poets. If I had been really serious about gaining distinction as a humorist, I should have emulated the porcine Rabelais, the bibulous Leacock, the Oscar Wilde who was such a physical disaster area that people got nauseated in his presence.

I blew it. Too many evenings with my ear glued to the radio, and the voice of Foster Hewitt pumping my heart full of *Hockey Night in Canada*.

Which is the greater thrill: to author a bestselling book or to win a tennis championship? I'd say that the exhilaration is about equal. The point is, doing both is possible only to a certain level of achievement. No one, to my knowledge, has both won Wimbledon and been named poet laureate. Baudelaire would have bombed as a poet had his dusky paramour been into volleyball. Can we picture Percy Bysshe Shelley running the Boston Marathon? (Yes, he did a bit of sailing, but obviously not too well.) As for Charles Dickens, like most other major writers, he did his aerobics in bed, with his wife or whomever he found a complete cardiovascular workout.

The cautionary message I draw from this ambivalence of focus in my life is that parents who wish to warp further the artistic bent of their child should not be content with breaking his or her arm. Wheelchair athletes can overcome most of the obstacles that once favoured the gimpy Lord Byron. Heroic measures are what today's parent must take:

1. Try to have a female child. Girls are heavily into athletics these days, but are less likely to dissipate their energy giving themselves a high five while watching *Monday Night Football*.

2. Feed the child a protein-free diet. Fill him/her up with fats, sugar, junk food of any kind, washed down by a cheap domestic wine. Pat the kid's paunch admiringly. Display alarm if she/he develops a muscle anywhere on the body. Encourage

her/him to decorate the walls of his/her room with poster pictures of Toulouse-Lautrec, Grandma Moses, Stan Laurel...

3. Make the child wear glasses, whether the kid needs them or not. Thick spectacles of breakable glass automatically exclude a boy or girl from many competitive sports such as hockey or baseball. Tell the kid that studies have shown that contact lenses eventually slice off the eyelids, and he will never be able to blink again.

4. Discourage your child from attending major sports events. Hero worship of a star athlete like Wayne Gretzky, adulation made visible to the kid in the stands, can be fatal to nurturing the degraded body and dissolute habits requisite for distinction as a contemporary novelist, or even a journalist. Author Norman Mailer, who once displayed a trace of athleticism by slugging his wife in the stomach, was an anomaly, somewhat pathetic in his effort to be an all-rounder.

5. Force your child to join a team in a minor league that plays some sport that the child doesn't much care for, then stand on the sideline and bully the kid for flubbing a catch or missing a check. A five-year-old encased in protective hockey, football or baseball gear, wearing a uniform and number before he has learned to count, may be fairly expected to loathe all team games before he is fifteen. The youngster is ready to become fully effeminate (unless a girl), and gladly register for ballet classes.

In these respects I did have some advantages as a potential writer:

1. For playing fields we had only the vacant lot, or the street. My parents never came to watch me play anything.

2. We played our games in the same shirts and shorts we wore to school. No uniforms. Peer esteem did not depend on what we wore on our heads and our feet.

3. A coach was something attached to a locomotive. We were not like the rich Hollywood movie star's kid who, impressed by seeing another kid climb a tree, demanded, "Who's your coach?"

Thanks in part to these limitations, I found time for writing. This took the form of unsigned pieces for the school paper, the *Scarlet and Grey*. These provided an outlet for the exhibitionism denied me by my not making the school's cricket team. (I flunked white flannels.) I also found delight in writing silly letters to practically anyone willing to open the envelope. The person didn't need to be in absentia. I would be a pun-wielding pen pal to anything that moved *or* stayed in town.

Then, suddenly, the Depression grabbed me by the short and curlies. Just days after I graduated from Lord Byng with first-class marks, my father lost his job with the brokerage firm which, in fact, had been caught in a scam that even the Vancouver Stock Exchange—one of the most broadminded in the world—could not countenance. My father called a family council meeting in our kitchen nook, where we normally ate the meals that I had taken for granted. He explained the situation to my mother and me, told us not to panic and announced that he proposed to return to the United Kingdom to study the feasibility of opening an auto court (motel) there. He was into another of his entrepreneurial phases, and that alone was enough to drain the blood from the faces of Mom and me.

I remember saying, "I won't go to university this fall. I'll find a job." My voice was lower for my having swallowed a lead ingot. Four years of grinding for the marks that made me number two in each grade—down the tube. I tried to be a little soldier about absorbing these slings and arrows of outrageous fortune, but every fibre of my body cried out for surrender to outright wailing against the injustice of a time that was out of joint while my father was out of work, and my being born to set it right by getting a job. My parents assured me that I would not be required to make the supreme sacrifice. But in their faces I saw it writ large: ruin. No prospects higher than my earning a commission in the ranks of the unemployed. Sweet sixteen turned to vinegar.

My father left for England, clutching his belief that the Old Country was primed and ready for a court where the automobile was sovereign. My mother got a part-time job as a clerk in a dress shop, and I spent most of my days on the golf course, caddying. The Jericho Golf and Country Club was supported by wealthy professionals to whom the Depression was more of a nuisance than a devastation. Because I was a very junior caddy (the senior caddies got the big tippers such as the male doctors and lawyers), I had to be at the pro shack at dawn until after dusk to lug for the doctors' and lawyers' wives, the documented deadbeats, or the ancient Scots who expected their caddy to retrieve their balls from the water hazard, regardless of whether he could swim or the water was the Pacific Ocean.

The Jericho golf course was engineered by a sadist who made the most of the steep hills and gullies that nature provided on the Point Grey peninsula. Double-bagged by two sets of clubs belonging to members of a ladies' foursome, I developed the hump of an overworked camel. I would stumble through the sand of bunkers, beat the rough for a refugee golf ball apparently valued as a family heirloom, or just teeter with fatigue while the ladies chose a new topic of gossip with which to approach the green that seemed to me ever to recede into the sunset.

On one of the few times that I was privileged to caddy for a man, he wrathfully chewed me out for letting my shadow fall across the path of his putt which, of course, he missed by several feet. Vampires and caddies—both are terrified of the sun.

In a distressingly short time my father returned from the United Kingdom, having needed only a couple of weeks there to determine that the British were not disposed toward the concept of the motel, the market being firmly sewed up by the bed-and-breakfast and the Fawlty Towers-type of seaside hotel. Aside from sleeping and eating, the English had no use for an inn—a sad commentary on the sexual mores of that uptight little isle. I was being shafted by their limited purpose of accommodation.

Luckily my father's savings for a rainy day held out until the ill wind of the Great Depression blew him into a job with the aborning Unemployment Insurance Commission, a niche he occupied until his retirement in 1958. Thus mine was one of the earliest mouths to find a teat on our wonderful welfare state.

However, my admission to first-year University of British Columbia was a bit rich for the family exchequer. All that caddying had earned me only part of the $148 registration fee. In the fall of 1937 my academic future hung in the balance while my application for a bursary—$100 offered by the Imperial Order of the Daughters of the Empire to children of war veterans—was scrutinized by the university's grants committee.

Feeling guilty about trying to cash in on the horror of World War I, I was required to take a means test in the form of an oral inquisition before three university administrators. They sat as a triumvirate of humiliation on the bench before me, while I badmouthed my family's standard of living. Here my appearance conspired against me. Mom's custard pies and rice puddings had plumped me up to a traitorously well-fed 190 pounds on a five-foot-ten-inch frame. I tried to think thin, but I could see in the frosty countenances of the judges that I failed to exhibit the degree of emaciation requisite to being granted the IODE bursary.

Yet I got it. Maybe the first choice died of malnutrition before he could claim it. Anyway, I paid over the first-term fee of $74 and—to complete my season of mortification—painted my fingernails green and donned a green skullcap as required of freshmen at UBC in that primal era. The barbaric rites of initiation are about all that I remember of my first year in arts. My main concern was to avoid being tossed into the library reflecting pool by the ravaging hordes of engineers. Water pollution was not the environmental concern that it is today, and I saw several of my fellow Class of '41 members summarily dumped into the long-suffering *bassin*.

The culmination of Frosh Week, Bonfire Night, was equally horrific. It was the social occasion when a huge stack of timbers was mounded on the vacant lot that later supported the Faculty of Law building. Ringing the pyre, sophomores defied the efforts of the frosh to set it afire.

This evoked full-scale war. Fire hoses were recruited from buildings. Fire bombs were hurled. People got burned (one chap disfigured for life). And there I was, crawling up and down a muddy trench, praying for my introduction to higher learning to stop making an ash of itself.

This violence was fairly routine in a time when the Spanish Civil War raged, Japan was bombing China's port cities, and Stalin was murdering his own people in the Soviet Union. Not a period conducive to the cloistered life of scholarship.

My chosen discipline, commerce, introduced me to the occult world of economics. This I found to be even more bewildering than the mysteries of sex. The Depression had shaken faith in capitalism so profoundly that any student who was not a militant socialist, if not a closet Communist, could be declared clinically brain-dead. Although I felt no emotional involvement with the birth of the Co-operative Commonwealth Federation—something that happened to Prairie farmers left with no topsoil—I did feel righteous indignation when I got a second-class grade for Economics 100, a blot on my first-year average. I immediately switched career goals from economist to teacher of French. The options were few in those days. If one's bent was not toward engineering (and the hair of my high school woodwork instructor turned white after a year of watching me abuse lumber), or agriculture (milking a cow struck me as an imposition for both parties), then the arts degree at least carried a ticket to a livelihood in teaching. Also, Dr. Dallas (French 100) had great legs.

Despite the fanatical pursuit of the high marks needed to qualify me for another bursary or scholarship, I did experience some intellectual stirrings. I discovered Bernard Shaw and Bertrand Russell, and was able to identify myself as a freethinker. Equally exhilarating was my learning that the campus club called the Student Christian Movement was a front for left-wing radicals, and the coven of the sexiest, wildest coeds to cross the quad. They were, I heard, attracted by the Leninist doctrine of free love. I was sorely tempted to become a nominal Christian in order to share in this personally relevant application of "from each according to his abilities, to each according to his needs." However, it offended my intellectual integrity to embrace Marx and Christ simultaneously, just to get closer to that redhead in Chemistry 100.

Agnosticism. That was the unorthodox religion that lit a candle in the darkness of my soul, or where my soul would have been if I had one. My best friend in high school had been a Jewish lad named Sam Stone. One day, when my father was driving us both someplace, he got irate at another driver and shouted, "You damn Jew!" This gaffe, after my father and I got home, led to a nasty exchange that further soured relations between us, and strengthened my skepticism about the Christian God—good, bad or indifferent? As an agnostic who accepted the existence of an unknowable Creator and the useful principles of a teacher named Jesus, I avoided the extremes of atheism and popery. I didn't believe in Heaven or Hell, but if I died and found that I was wrong—toasty wrong—I would have grounds for an appeal because the Creator gave me a weak sense of the supernatural.

However, there was no Agnostics Club at UBC. Since I had not been rushed by any of the fraternities—their spotting system having quickly eliminated both the solitary and those who saved bus fare by biking to the campus—I had no hope of becoming a Greek, with all that this promised by way of panty raids and other entrées to carnal congress.

So I put my craving for attention on paper: I wrote an anonymous column for the student paper, *The Ubyssey*. Flaunting tight-fitting puns, I was sublimating the male courting display by showing off my figure of speech. If the two most satisfying sounds that a man can evoke from a woman are the moan of ecstasy and the hoot of laughter, I went for the giggle. For starters.

Writing the *Ubyssey* column, I experienced the buzz of *publication*, not merely the blotchy, mimeographed sheets of the *Scarlet and Grey*, but actual print on paper that one could take with confidence into the university washroom. For most people the narcotic effect of publication is nonaddictive. They are satisfied with the occasional letter to the editor, or a graffito on the wall of the toilet cubicle. But others—far too many of us, as any publisher will attest—are hooked for life. Having once seen our words in print, we seek the ever-greater rush of readership. The privacy of the personal diary doesn't gratify us unless we are popping Pepys. Full many a flower may be born to blush unseen, and waste its sweetness on the desert air, but Thomas Gray went to some trouble to get *his* blooms into the florist's window.

The *Ubyssey* column that spaced me out was an Asian drug called "Chang Suey." Created during the 1920s and sustained by the irreverent likes of poet Earle Birney, Suey was a highly fictitious Chinese detective whose berserk adventures on the campus lampooned members of the faculty, student council and virtually anything else that deserved respect. The anonymity of authorship appealed to me, as did the fact that the column was used as a filler, written by anyone the editors judged to be too incompetent to serve as a reporter or identifiable columnist. The Pub (Publication Office) was a den of battered desks and spastic typewriters, redolent of peeled oranges and undone homework, where recruited freshettes discovered the moral standards of the white-slave markets of Marrakech.

Me, I slipped into the Pub like a wraith, dropped "Chang Suey" into the copy basket and was gone before anyone could identify the author and recommend psychiatric treatment. The column quickly found a following among students and staff in need of an absurdity less menacing than Hitler's moustache. It gave me great pleasure to lead the double life: the solemn, book-cracking grades chaser, and the writer of manic rubbish that just happened to relieve some tension in a world preparing for war.

The senior editor of the *Ubyssey* was a rangy, redheaded extrovert from the Yukon named Pierre Berton, who was using his northern expertise to cure frigidity in his female reporters. I appreciated Pierre's giving me, in my junior year, a regular column called "The Mummery" and bylined "Jabez" (Hebrew for "He will give pain," and a craven cover).

Pierre and I never really hit it off socially. I didn't drink, and if Pierre didn't, he wisely gave no evidence of sobriety. The Pub parties had a reputation to uphold as the most lubricated of any campus student organization. Even when patently sober, Pierre had such galvanic energy that, despite his meteoric rise in Pub editorial, he would, in my assessment, burn himself out before graduation, and never truly amount to anything.

I also believed that Adolf Hitler was just bluffing.

Up until 1939, though I had some doubts about God, my faith in Neville Chamberlain, the British prime minister, was complete and unconditional. After all, his moustache outranked Hitler's. And when he returned, beaming, from Munich, waving a bit of paper and declaring "peace in our time," I bought it. I had to. My French Honours course had

In Loving Memory
of
JABEZ
(Eric P. Nicol)
Beloved campus humorist who for
a full decade gave
to his fellow men the priceless
gift of laughter.
1937 - 1947

Why University of BC students assume I died fifty years ago. (BCBW)

me up to my hips in Molière and Pascal, which was as close as I wanted to get to France at that moment. I had made such a heavy investment in higher education that I had no trouble convincing myself that Adolf and Benito were basically reasonable chaps. A tad flamboyant perhaps in burning down the Reichstag and bombing those spear-waving Ethiopians but, hell, nobody's perfect.

In the summer of 1939, while the Nazi panzer divisions prepared to pummel Poland, I was fully occupied with earning enough money to pay for university. With his forestry connections my father helped me get one of the rare jobs— as a spark chaser with the Port Renfrew Logging operation on the rugged west coast of Vancouver Island. This was my first experience of being away from home, on my own, and among some rather rough gentlemen who viewed university students as on a par with the spruce budworm, i.e., a seasonal pest. They were best eliminated by putting 100-pound tanks of water on their backs and telling them to climb 1,500 feet up a mountainside covered with logging debris.

I might have been eradicated early had not the summer turned abnormally soggy, obviating the need for a spark chaser to monitor the fires started by rubbing two sticks together—each stick weighing several tons. I was assigned to work in the timekeeper's hut, helping him keep his books and minding the counter of the small commissary. Abruptly I became a storekeeper. My first year of commerce stood me in poor stead. My customers were exclusively male, usually large and rarely in a sportive mood after a long day's battle with the outback. Deprived for months on end of the comfort that only a woman can give, they had a fierce need of something else that was soft and sweet and chewable: gum, candies and snoose. Until I became a backwoods shopkeeper, Copenhagen had been only a city in Denmark. Port Renfrew instructed me in the mystique of chewing tobacco, as the spit and image of other than baseball players. What is it, I wonder, about moving lumber that encourages sucking a cud? Is there something about absorbing nicotine through the gums that helps to prevent getting beaned by a flying object?

I slept in the tiny storeroom on a cot beside a window that was only a few feet from the railway track used by the locomotives hauling logs from the upper camp to the lower. When the window was open, the loco's burst of live steam blew through it. I never needed a shower. I was dry-cleaned. This luxury was offset, though, by the floor's flea-infested sawdust, which made standing in one place for more than five seconds an invitation to pernicious anemia.

The following summer I was back, packing flea powder as

all I needed to make my workplace completely congenial.

I got a rude shock.

Instead of ushering me into my private room, the Push (superintendent) informed me that I would be doing my initial job: spark chasing in the woods. The weather had betrayed me. The woods were dry. Combustion, if not spontaneous, was certainly feasible.

The Push took me personally to the upper camp in his track car—an old auto whose tires had been replaced with rail wheels. The steering wheel was superfluous. So, I felt, was I. Barrelling along, sharing the single track with a logging locomotive that could appear suddenly around the next bend, did not impress me as an improvement over any form of transport except possibly the tumbrel.

Worse awaited at the upper camp where the fallers and buckers—the front line of the war against the environment—were crowded into bunkhouses that would make a Spartan general blanch. I was assigned to one of these by the foreman, a big, mean-looking immigrant from some land where life is cheap. He took an immediate dislike to me. The foreman's house, up the side of a hill above the bunkhouse area, was accessible only by about 100 feet of wooden steps that no man trod but the owner. The reason: the foreman's wife was the only woman allowed in a camp of thirty or forty men. The foreman guarded her with a flint-edged paranoia that made it highly unlikely that I would be invited up for tea, regardless of my qualifications to discuss the French Romantic poets.

I was put to chasing sparks immediately. Herded into a crummy (a boxcar unfit for horses), the crew was taken to the cut site, where I staggered up the mountain with my backpack of spark extinguisher. My attention to smouldering logs was distracted somewhat by something I had overheard in the crummy conversation: bears were active around the cutting site. One big female with cubs had chased a road-building crew, which had to throw dynamite caps at the animal to stave off her charge. Charming. I had not been issued with dynamite caps, or a change of underwear.

I also had no hard hat. The bush-league chapeau was seen as sissified in that era of logging. Your skull was on its own. The fact that my hair was standing on end was minimum protection. If I met a bear, my best hope was that she would be very thirsty and grateful for my squirting water into her mouth. With luck the bear would not consider this libation as an aperitif to be followed by a meal that my mother had prepared: me.

After spending the long morning stumbling over logs and dodging cables that whizzed through the brush like snakes avid to amputate a limb—arboreal or human—I joined the crew opening lunch buckets. Almost at once two bears came crashing out of the bush, a big one led by a smaller, pilot bear, honing in on the scent of beef sandwiches. The other guys were accustomed to these piggy-eyed panhandlers, and tossed scraps in their direction before returning to work.

"They don't like the noise of the skidder," a chokerman explained to me, and indeed the animals did retreat into the woods.

At four in the afternoon the quitting whistle blew. However, my orders were to remain up the hill for half an hour after the rest of the crew had returned to the crummy and back to camp, my purpose being to ensure that no fire was smouldering in the slash. The crummy had barely disappeared down the track before I heard, and recognized, the crashing of ursine bodies returning to the scene. And out they lumbered, Mutt and Jeff. What had been an amusing novelty when I was in the company of ten or fifteen burly loggers became an entirely different situation for someone alone and aware that a bear can outrun a man, outclimb a man and, in my case, outlive a man.

I still had thirty minutes to go on my watch. As the bears circled me—a bear's eyesight is not great but the animal has an exquisite sense of smell—the dilemma on whose horns I was impaled was: ought I cut short my vigil, and thereby give the foreman the excuse he needed to send me packing back to town, or should I try to stare down a brace of bruins on their own turf? They were slowly zeroing in on my empty lunch bucket. I considered throwing them the pail, but when they found it devoid of food would they not be peeved enough to order sun-ripened greenhorn à la carte?

I compromised, with a slow withdrawal down the hill that only the picky would call a retreat. Moving a few yards at a time, and inspired by self-preservation, I jumped atop one of the fresh stumps and burst into song. "O Canada!" I bellowed at the bears. "We stand on guard for thee!" The bears halted, visibly shaken by an acoustic horror beyond their ken. My singing voice has much the same effect on humans. I pressed my advantage and let the bears have an earful: "God save our gracious king!" I don't say that the bears reeled. But if I hadn't destroyed their appetite, I had surely made them think about the high price they were paying to satisfy it.

I fell back to another stump. "Onward Christian soldiers, marching as to war!" I could see that this was making a diet of berries and honey look pretty good. Although the bears didn't actually throw up, their heads were bobbing as though the flow of gastric juices had definitely turned sour.

I was into a full-throated chorus of "Old Man River" when I reached the bottom of the hill, and the railway track.

Luckily the speeder sent to fetch me arrived five minutes early. The driver looked at me quizzically, having caught the last few bars of my vocal. But I didn't mention the bears, suddenly feeling very tired, and closer than ever to Virginia Woolf.

Revising an essay on Virginia Woolf was my after-hours project at the logging camp, where I got access to the first-aid shack. The essay had won the UBC English Department Book Prize, and the department head, Dr. G.G. Sedgewick, considered it worthy of publication.

One of the greatest teachers ever to be lost from the legitimate stage, Dr. Sedgewick held forth on Shakespeare's plays to the delight and edification of generations of UBC students. A dapper, diminutive figure, head too large for his body, hankie tucked into the jacket cuff, red bow tie vibrating on a resonant throat, sometimes delivering Hamlet's soliloquy while reclining on the table, G.G. placed the huge football players in the front seats of the lecture hall so that he could emphasize points by striking their beetled brows with his tiny fist. The hulks often responded by carrying the prof bodily to his office, legs thrashing in mock objection.

On the strength of my screed on Virginia Woolf, Dr. Sedgewick invited me to his Kitsilano home for tea. A bachelor, he lived alone with his housekeeper, who brought us our tray and disappeared. For half an hour G.G. quizzed me about my personal habits and my relationships while he paced the drawing room with increasing agitation as my answers failed—for some reason inscrutable to me—to satisfy him. When at last I left, I could tell I had somehow flunked a test not listed on the course examinations. Only much later did it dawn on me why: I was not gay.

Chapter 7

From Beast of Burden to Baccalaureate

I was unable to finish revising the Virgina Woolf essay at the logging camp that summer of 1941 because my fingers seized up. The woods had again become too wet to need spark chasing, so the foreman found me an alternative method of suicide.

"You help build house," he instructed me. In his eyes I could see the hope that my clambering around crossbeams would do the job the bears failed to. The house was being built on an earth terrace bulldozed from the side of a hill, up which all the lumber had to be lugged by unskilled and therefore expendable members of the workforce. I met the criteria.

For the next week, under skies suddenly turned hot and cloudless, I learned something of what the building of Egypt's pyramids involved by way of isometric delight for the slaves hauling the blocks of stone. No whips were used on us, but I was goaded by the smirks of my fellow pack animals, browned and burly brutes who could carry lengths of two-by-fours three at a time, while I buckled under two.

"You new boy?" one of them asked, grinning at me.

Maddening. By the end of the day I was blistered from nose to heel. When I woke in the morning, my hands were frozen into claws, the tendons having gone into shock. I pried my fingers open, pulled on the boots whose tongues were still hanging out from carrying the freight, and lurched back to the lumber-piles that even Preparation H couldn't shrink fast enough to relieve my pain. But I didn't cry. Getting the Strap had prepared me for this.

When at last the studs and siding were all atop the building site, the foreman told me to assist the camp carpenter, Wes Harper, a giant of a man with a Falstaffian sense of humour and enormous zest for life—my life. He loomed as final retribution for my performance in Manual Training, where I learned nothing but how to cut corners. While other students were making breadboards and letter holders, I was making sawdust, using only a hammer and a screwdriver. My manual training teacher, a dour North Country Englishman, regarded me with a mixture of awe and fear, as though I were an oversize type of termite escaped from central Africa and fully capable of destroying most of British Columbia's timber export.

I was living the First Law of Acadynamics: the subject in which you are weakest in school is the one most needed when you get a job.

Wes Harper greeted my ineptitude with uproarious laughter.

He never let me near his saws. I was his gofer, fetching other material up and down ladders and teetering across stringers. Once, when the ladder slipped from under me and left me dangling over a twenty-foot drop, Harper's reaction was prompt: "Ha, ha, ha! Shit your pants, eh, Curly?"

I had not shit my pants. Intimidated by the camp's ten-hole latrine, my bowels were taking the summer off. I remember eating well, but have no recollection of crapping for six weeks.

When it was getting to be time to return to town, I overheard Wes Harper tell the foreman, "That kid's the hardest-workin' bugger you got here." At last! I'd come first in something.

On the evening of my last man-making day, that summer of '41, the Port Renfrew monthly dance was held in the community recreation hall. I poked my nose in the door of the shuddering building, but quickly withdrew. It was a terrifying sight: boozed-up loggers wearing cleat boots thundering through the polka with women rounded up from somewhere, anywhere, including the nearby Indian reserve. I could now understand why only one stringer was needed for the log-dump ramp but two stringers were required to support the dance hall.

"Curly!" God, he had spotted me. Not only did I not know how to dance, and had never attended a dance, but having survived an assault by bears and house building, I was damned if I was going to die in a backwoods ballroom.

"Curly!" I had a glimpse of Harper flinging away his partner and charging toward me like a rogue elephant. Was he going to ask me to dance with him? The thought put wings on my heels. I ran, ran, ran, stopping in the darkness of the railway track. From there I saw Harper reel out of the door of the hall and stand at the top of the steps, where he pounded his chest and yelled, "Curly! Watch a man who can piss and get a hard on at the same time!"

I was not disposed to serve as spectator for this urethral feat. I believed him. Instead I took off down the track at pace, not stopping until I was huddled in my bunk, a constipated Cinderella.

This was to be the last night of my one, and only, experience of working in one of Canada's primary resource industries. It left me with a bad impression of what we do for a living. To be part of clearcut logging, an entire mountainside defaced and bleeding sawdust as red as an open wound, the joyless rape of forest by teams of men whose only purpose there was to get "stakey," get out to town, and get very drunk with an Indian hooker—how could I wonder that British Columbia is a bloody-minded province?

That said, my brush with forest management did leave me with an abiding respect for the courage of the men—and they are, still, mostly men despite women's liberation—who daily risk death or injury in order to produce the paper for people like me to abuse. In my opinion every student of creative writing should be required to spend at least one summer working in the woods so that he may return to his classes inspired to write shorter novels and pithier poems.

I returned home with my stake of $175 and as randy as a goat on locoweed. Sensing that my parents would not approve of my relieving myself of either by hiring a whore, I felt that I had returned victorious from a battle without the raping and pillaging that once were the standard reliefs for young men's lust, but now socially unacceptable. I was reluctant to do anything that would make me hate myself in the morning. A mild dislike, yes, that I'd accept. But none of the options offered other than acute self-loathing.

We have prearranged mortgages, prearranged tours of

Europe, prearranged funerals, but no prearranged sex for the teenager who still wants to feel good about himself. Surely this is cruel and unnatural punishment for being young. Would it not be more humane if parents could offer their son a gift certificate to an escort service whose instructors were licensed as social workers? Improvisation may be fun in the theatre, but not in the real world where a lad already strumming his lip is constantly exposed to frighteningly healthy young women wearing nothing but a designer loin-cloth.

(I have no panacea to suggest for teenage girls. I see them standing on their heads a lot, but I'm not sure that it is orgasmic.)

For me the focus of craving was a stripper named Gypsy Rose Lee. Decades later, as a *Province* columnist, I interviewed Gypsy in her dressing room at the Cave nightclub in Vancouver. She was demurely wrapped in an old robe and wanted to talk about the two dachshunds that travelled with her and had learned to go potty in hotel toilets. It was a dreadful letdown for this votary, who had first met her photographed in black bra and panties in a grainy magazine I found in the gutter where it doubtless belonged. This picture stimulated an appetite for which there was no proper diet: I became a burlesque junkie.

Impossible to calculate are the millions of man-hours lost because of Minsky fever that raged through North America during the 1930s. The burlesque circuit brought to Vancouver the world's greatest exotic dancers. I saw them all. Why a guy would spend good money (25 cents) to be teased unmercifully must be one of the larger mysteries of adolescence, whether delayed or right on time. Grown men still, I'm told, frequent hotel bars where young women writhe in the altogether, take showers they don't need and otherwise titillate the voyeur in the lamentable male psyche. *Plus ça change...*

But the burlesque that graced the stage of Vancouver's old Beacon Theatre in the city's tenderloin district on Hastings Street was an artistic cut above today's rather rudimentary lap dancing. It was a *show.* Vaudeville and a movie, maybe a double feature, which I sat through impatiently, waiting for the Unveiling. To get a good seat near the front—but not in the bald-headed row where my youthful thatch would stand out—I went to the early matinees, when most of the other patrons were elderly Chinese gentlemen from nearby Chinatown. Inscrutable, totally unresponsive to the most vigorous bumps and grinds, this audience was the despair of the stand-up comedians whose jokes rolled down the aisles like tumbleweed in the desert.

Inadvertently the burlesque comedy acts—usually either the classic courtroom scene where the baggy-panted lawyer enters carrying a ladder ("I'm taking the case to a higher court"), or the patient in the doctor's office ("Have you ever had this pain before?" "Yes, Doctor." "Then you've got it again.")—introduced me to the one-liner as a desperate means of livelihood, that of the gag writer. Latent education.

What absorbed me more at the time, though, was the dimming of the blue lights that introduced the star attraction: Sally Rand, or Gypsy Rose Lee, or Ann Corio, or Tempest Storm, or Canada's own Lily St. Cyr, as well as lesser astral bodies like Tessie the Tassel Twirler and the ever-lovely Hard-Hearted Hannah. These were a constellation of such magnitude that H.L. Mencken coined a name to honour it: *ecdysiast*, from the Greek word for "putting off." But what I learned, of more practical use than the stately bounce of Sally's big (*too* damn big) bubble, was the rhythms of line comedy. Maybe the Chinese gentlemen also picked up a few pointers on the use of the fan.

Even before I was old enough to be sidling along Skid Road to the Beacon in order to gratify an insatiable hunger to watch shapely women say naughty things in body language, my parents had taken me to uptown vaudeville at the magnificent Orpheum Theatre. An even richer vein of vintage comedy, the Orpheum circuit brought me the giants in that time of great comedy acts: Burns and Allen, Wheeler and Wolsey, the Ritz Brothers, Olsen and Johnson's *Hellzapoppin*. All of them had their own exquisitely honed devices for making an audience pee its pants, which was made manifest to me. Unconsciously I absorbed the message that humour can be the headiest form of crowd control available to a person without using a water cannon.

What power! To make untold numbers of people explode air from their lungs, clutch one another, collapse helplessly, tears coursing down their cheeks! Such amiable tyranny! Combine that with a young person too shy to go onstage in person, and one has the makings of a benign despot—the humorist.

By 1941 it was becoming plain that the war in Europe would not be over by Christmas 1939, as I had been led to believe. With the fall of France, the Dunkirk evacuation of Allied troops and the bombing blitz on Britain, there was increasing pressure on the Mackenzie King government to enact conscription and revoke the special status of university students. The nation was now prepared to risk brain damage, including this good grey cell entering his graduate year. I had already exchanged my logging-camp boots for those of a cadet in the UBC contingent of the Canadian Officers Training Corps (COTC). Every able-bodied student was issued a khaki uniform and required to drill once a week.

Our commanding officer was Colonel Gordon Shrum, a tall, balding man, veteran of World War I, now head of the university's physics department. I had never understood physics in high school, and I failed to understand Colonel Shrum, though he had a voice that carried for hundreds of yards and left a crater where it landed.

Since the Canadian army couldn't spare us equipment needed by its real soldiers, our training consisted chiefly of route marches through the University Endowment Lands, the colonel heading up the brown millipede, and the rear ranks chanting, "Shrum's a bum...Shrum's a bum..." in a failing effort to keep the cadence. Our other officers were professors drafted from various disciplines, my favourite being our security officer, charged with thwarting Nazi spies from discovering that Canada's officer material had ravelled. Dr. Geoffrey Riddehough was head of the classics department, a roly-poly little man who, despite his being an international authority on Homer, had no sense of rhythm whatever, so that his footwork at the head of a company of men guaranteed marching chaos. I believe that Shrum kept the route march away from populated areas for fear of lowering morale—among the civilians.

The totality of the folly of commissioning academics as army officers became apparent at the COTC spring field camp, held in an unsuspecting cow pasture near Nanaimo on Vancouver Island. Granted, we accomplished the landing with only a few minor casualties (one lad fell off the ferry gangplank). But the list of walking wounded swelled when we tried to fit the square-rigged marquees on round wooden floors made for Bell tents. The floor of every tent looked like a jigsaw puzzle put together by a retarded Fate. With heavy rains sluicing through the misfits, a restless sleeper could roll off his palliasse and debouch into Nanaimo harbour, an unidentified floating object.

The commerce professor who was in charge of Stores proved his competence to be purely theoretical when the troops sat down to our first supper: lettuce and raspberry jam. Mountains of lettuce and cases of jam had arrived, but nothing vaguely resembling protein. There are few ways that even the cleverest cook can disguise a jam salad to make it appetizing, and our cooks—transvestite home economics majors—gave up the fight even faster than France. It was not until the third day of camp that other food supplies started to trickle in, by which time most of us cadets had switched our hatred from Hitler to greens. If this man's army was to march on its stomach, it would be looping along like an inchworm.

I did not accept these glitches like a little soldier. Instead, I sneaked off to Nanaimo and a good restaurant, where a pair of officers caught me scoffing up sausage and mashed. Nor did my ineptitude in handling men impress my superiors favourably. I did not bark orders well, my tone being conciliatory rather than authoritarian. Sometimes I was downright apologetic, after marching my squad into a wall.

During attack manoeuvres in the field, I always seemed to be crawling behind my comrades in arms, my map reading then, as now, being such that I could get my unit lost to the point of leaving the entire theatre of operations. I even flunked guard duty, allowing through the gate any vehicle that did not appear disposed to stop when I waved my arms.

I failed the course. Not officer material. My mark indicated that the grading officers felt that it would be preferable to surrender to the Axis powers rather than to put a pip on my shoulder.

An exhausted, sun-blistered corps stumbled back onto the ferry to Vancouver, arriving back on the campus just in time for the graduation ceremony, where I nodded off until my name was called for admission as a bachelor of arts, with award of the French Government Silver Medal, as well as the Graduate Scholarship for second-best average after the winner of the Governor General's Medal. My immediate prospects: to be one of the best-educated young men ever to qualify as cannon fodder.

I didn't fancy my chances as a combatant in World War II. Having graduated with a first in French Honours, I would be a prime candidate to be parachuted into France, get hopelessly lost and establish a new record for the shortest elapsed time between leaving Britain and being shot by the Germans as a remarkably inept spy. I felt that if it is true that whom the gods love die young, then Zeus must have a real crush on me.

Fortunately I was able to put the assignation on hold. The COTC expanded its training to include pre-aircrew for the Royal Canadian Air Force. I seized on the chance to follow in the fly-path of my illustrious second cousin, Major Mick Mannock, V.C., D.S.O., M.C., greatest Allied fighter pilot of World War I. Maybe it was in the genes, the lightning reflexes and killer instinct of the top Ping-Pong player. Even if I, too, got shot down in flames, it would be because *I* erred, not because some buck-toothed English officer twit pointed his swagger stick in the wrong direction.

Having passed the medical, I was soon into a program of navigation, meteorology and other prerequisites to putting paid to the Red Baron Mark 2. At the same time I started my M.A. thesis and, possibly a bit hysterical from these discordant studies, I wrote my first stage play. A one-act farce entitled *Her Scienceman Lover*, this slender work was presented by the Players Club as a noon-hour fund-raiser in the university Auditorium. In hindsight the cast was illustrious, including as it did Lister Sinclair, Arthur Hill and Norman Campbell, each of whom was destined for distinguished careers in entertainment.

Lister, even as a university undergraduate, had the polished aspect and manner of the born intellectual. Supremely urbane, he used his cane as a prop for his debonair wit. I was awed by his gift for storytelling, and still remember his flawless delivery of one joke.

A madam is pitching her Vancouver brothel to a potential customer. "And we cater only to distinguished white gentlemen in my establishment," she says. At that moment an obviously Oriental client shuffles by, outward bound and buttoning his fly. "Ah!" says the madam. "The Chinese ambassador to Canada!"

Whereas Lister looked a worldly fifty when he was twenty, Norm Campbell remained frosh-faced until proven otherwise. Which he was, of course, co-authoring with Don Harron the most popular stage musical ever produced in Canada—*Anne of Green Gables*.

I drop Norman's name with full confidence that it was the role in *Her Scienceman Lover* that lit the fire of theatrical talent, and he owes me two tickets, front row, in Charlottetown.

Her Scienceman Lover gave me my first chance to sit at the back of the house and inhale the heady fumes of an audience laughing at my stuff. I was snorting a substance as addictive as cocaine and probably more hazardous to my health. The play was revived every year, becoming progressively smuttier as the cast improvised new lines until at last it became too gamey to be brought indoors.

Almost simultaneously with the performance of my play, Japan bombed Pearl Harbor on December 7, 1941. Historians have found no connection between the two events. But both

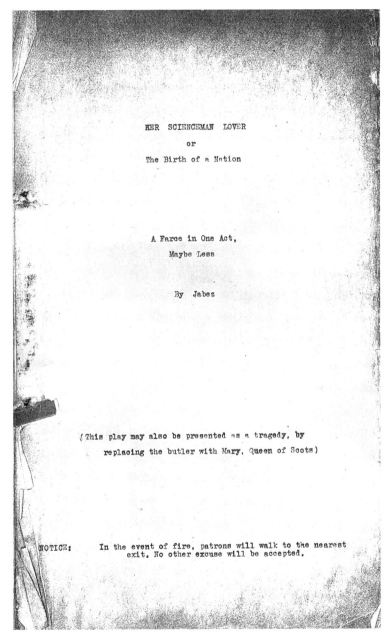

Opus #1, introduction to "the roar of the greasepaint, the smell of the crowd," 1941. (UBC)

got my attention. With most of the US Pacific Fleet smouldering hulks in Hawaii, the ocean belonged to the Japanese Imperial Fleet. Abruptly, from being a quiet retreat for academia, the Point Grey campus lay at the tip of the peninsula where the "Japs" would swarm ashore, storm the cliffs and find the UBC contingent of the COTC lined up in the Armouries, waiting for Stores to issue us white flags.

At the base of the cliff fronting our Botanical Gardens, the Department of Defence installed the concrete emplacement for a single artillery piece, whose function would be to delay Japanese warships from entering English Bay for about five minutes, or long enough for their dive bombers to take out that bunker and several other bunkers on the University Golf Course. Meantime the blackout added to the hazard of riding a bike home, and the westerly wind that formerly boded only fair weather now bore the drifting Japanese fire-bomb balloons, with which the enemy hoped to set ablaze enough of British Columbia's forests to barbecue all resistance. In the event, only a few flammatory balloons were found to have reached the coast, but at the time my father stood ready every night with his ARP helmet, and in our basement the stirrup pump and buckets of sand that spoke for our resolve to survive any fiery holocaust on Point Grey.

Yes, war is Hell.

Chapter 8

The Belated First Date

"**E**at, drink and be merry for tomorrow we die." That was my agenda as the date for enlistment for active service drew nearer. I was already eating well. As for drink, Delaware Punch, though nonalcoholic, I found festive. But my being merry sexually needed work. I craved a woman who knew how to laugh and do other things with me that would make me less resentful about dying as a virgin.

To facilitate my chances, I paid $15 for a series of dance lessons. A disaster. The first time I put my arm around the waist of the attractive dance instructor, certain highly localized involuntary muscles sprang to life. The instructor didn't seem to mind the levitation, but I found it impossible to concentrate on any movement below the knees. If this could happen with one fox-trot lesson, the waltz could get me arrested. I aborted the mission. I felt, and still feel, that ballroom dancing is an oxymoron. No young man is safe dancing anything more contiguous than the Roger de Coverley.

Then I got lucky. While holidaying with my parents on Bowen Island that summer, I strayed into the hotel's Ping-Pong room and watched a game being played by a tall, slim redhead and someone who never entered my field of vision. My introduction to this freckle-faced girl with a smile that turned my hamstrings to cooked spaghetti occurred when I retrieved a Ping-Pong ball from under the table.

Madge was a telephone operator in the Kerrisdale exchange, a part of Vancouver that has all the better numbers. In that era when the operator, not a dial or buttons, placed one's phone call, she was trained to speak in a low, modulated tone. For thousands of young men, making a phone call was better than never to have loved at all. Now I had a date with not only the Voice but all its admirable accessories, including a figure that would wrench a whimper from a brass Buddha.

Happily I had gained access to Madge and my father's car together in the summer of 1942. This opened up new and exciting vistas to a youth tired of standing on his neck. There was one catch. In the tradition of star-crossed lovers I had been captivated by a woman whose boyfriend had gone overseas with the Canadian army and could at any moment be projected into battle with the Wehrmacht. This posed an ethical dilemma for me, roughly equivalent to being torn apart by wild horses. While I could enjoy escorting Madge to movies and romantic strolls along Spanish Banks bathed in sunset, when we were sitting in the parked car, with my arm around her shoulders, my whole being was so shivered that my legs jittered uncontrollably.

"You're cold?" Madge asked me once, smiling with that damn feminine intuition that makes it hard for a man to do the decent thing.

"No, no! Just right!" And my knees drummed against the steering wheel.

Incredibly I sustained this painfully platonic relationship for the entire summer, though each time I drove Madge home the strain of immaculate leave-taking became more protracted, and must have made the neighbours think we were either cataleptic or married. Since the reason for my restraint was understood between us, Madge was finally moved to say, "You're one in a million." High praise indeed, but it did nothing to stop my legs from twitching.

As a rare fish, I might have joined the coelacanth, a species thought to be extinct, had not Madge intervened. One evening she abbreviated the good-nights by dropping her purse on the floor of the car, and in picking it up, she let her lips brush mine. This broke the lava dome. The volcano erupted with a rain of hot kisses that threatened the enamel on Madge's incisors. When she at last retreated into her house, her chin was livid with beard burn, proving to the world how destructive sexual assault can be, even though it never goes beyond the facial.

The first kiss. The next day I sent her a gift-wrapped, rosy McIntosh apple: "To the teacher from a grateful student." No, we never did consummate the affair. I had a date with a recruiting officer. And I learned later that Madge never did marry the soldier who had helped to ruin World War II for me.

Besides the osculatory initiation, I remember fondly the automobile of the time—the ne plus ultra of mobile boudoirs. Today's cars come with air bags in case of collision, but what a hazard to the really ardent swain! Okay, so we have the padded dash, the recessed door handle, to reduce injury to lovers. But bucket seats? Floor-mounted gearshifts? Lower roofs? *No rumble seat?* This is progress? (I say nothing about the decline of the garter belt, replaced by the postbellum panty hose that, along with the United Nations, proved unworkable in tight situations.)

Anyway, my father's car was a significant factor in the metamorphosis of the bookworm, chewing stolidly on the M.A. thesis in the UBC Library stacks, into a cabbage moth in a mild flutter over finally getting the message from the birds and the bees. And there was another taking to the air: that summer of '42 I was invited to write for Canadian Broadcasting Corporation Radio.

The Mother Corporation was then in the full flush of girl-hood, her kilowatted hormones all pumping furiously with drama series produced by the magisterial Andrew Allan, with Foster Hewitt enthralling the nation with "He shoots! He scores!" and with a variety show out of Vancouver called *Stag Party* that was the darling of the feisty network. The star and head writer of *Stag Party* was a sad-faced young comic named Alan Young, whom the show shot to fame with such velocity that he soon escaped the gravitational pull of Canada and landed in Hollywood. There he teamed up with Mr. Ed, the talking horse, to achieve a fame and for-tune typical of Canadian talent that takes the precaution of getting the hell out of its home and native land.

Young's sudden departure in mid-season created a script-ing crisis. The producer's desperate tossing of the job to me on the strength of a few college skits and columns was inter-preted by some members of the cast as part of a plot to induce more performers to volunteer for active service in Burma. Also, I was happy to work cheap. Would, in fact, have been glad to write this national prime-time variety program for free. This has been the basis of my reputation as a bargainer whose shrewdness rates with that of a cocker spaniel. While I entirely agree with Samuel Johnson that no man but a blockhead ever wrote except for money, it didn't take much for me to have my head blocked. Today, of course, the novice writer would join a union that firmly instructed him or her, under a very bright light, on minimum rates. But with *Stag Party* only the musicians in Harry Pryce's band had a union, with the result that, as sole writer of the show, I was making less than a horn player who had three bars in the whole half hour.

However, one wonders if Shakespeare would have written as well, or as much, had he been obliged to join the Tudor Playwrights Union. Will would have spent many hours sitting at a table with fellow dramatists, debating whether they should picket the Earl of Pembroke. He might even have been appointed public-relations officer for the guild, and instead of *Hamlet* we would have a file of letters to members of Parliament—to beef, or not to beef.

Untroubled by such organized concern for my being worthy of my hire, I joyously pounded out reams of continuity and comedy sketches for the remarkably talented cast that included Bernard Braden, Barbara Kelly, Fletcher Markle and Al Pearce. They, and singer Juliette, played to a live audience in capacious Studio A, while I sat up in the booth with the producer—often the ebullient Mavor Moore, making a brilliant recovery from being from Toronto—and the engineer. There I had my apprenticeship in the agony and the ecstasy of the gag writer. This booth ordeal is like being an expectant father who has to go into the delivery room every week to watch the birth of dozens of his little darlings, and be shattered when they are stillborn, wincing at the runt giggle, but knowing sheer bliss—brief but incomparable—

when a line comes out with a roar.

In this labour I came to depend heavily on the midwifery of our sound-effects man. From him I learned how radio is the ideal medium for the imagination, thanks to sound effects like the classic of Jack Benny's descending into his basement in order to access his vault—four hysterical minutes of nought but drawbridge being raised, heavy doors groaning, locks clanging, chains rattling. With just two minutes of dead air—the ultimate sound effect—Orson Welles convinced millions of people in the northeast United States that fire-breathing Martians had landed and barbied all transmission.

Comparatively television is a handicapped medium—too literal for words.

But my romance with radio was quickly put on hold. With most of the *Stag Party* company, including me, heading off to various branches of the armed services, I found another, temporary outlet for manic expression. Jack Scott, the brilliant columnist for the *Vancouver News-Herald*, invited me to write a guest column while he was away on holiday. In 1942 columnists were required to keep their space filled, regardless of vacation or any physical ailment short of rabies. To this feudal system I owed my big break: a chance to get the attention of the general reading public, the hairy brute at café counter or saloon bar, or just sitting on the john, scratching and belching, with the columnist denied the use of the few words (all obscene) that the reader is apt to recognize, and with his column's predictable fate of being used to wrap fish and chips, line a birdcage, train a puppy or light a fire at the opposite end of the time scale from an eternal flame.

I leaped at the chance, with enough success that the *News-Herald* continued to run my pieces in tandem with

Scott's. The combo was too serendipitous to be interrupted by a little thing like military service. Jack marched off to army camp armed with his portable, and I packed a survival kit of copy paper for the trip to the RCAF manning depot. The columns written by Sergeant Scott and Sergeant Nicol were later compiled in *Says We*, a book in violation of several service regulations regarding moonlighting in uniform. It was my first offence as a book author.

But the rest of war service promised to be a bit of a drag. For me World War II came at a bad time—while I was still alive. Not only alive but at the perfect age (twenty) to receive a first invitation to this unsocial engagement. Also, I was in good enough health to be accepted for the one occasion when rejection would have been very easy to live with. (Actually, my health was not as good as advertised. I learned much later that I had a double hernia—deceptive because the pubic bumps made a set I hated to break up.)

No, World War II did not fit in with my plans, not after fourteen years of battling the books for top grades. Others might volunteer happily for the excitement, for the employment, or simply to escape a spouse who made Mussolini look winsome, but not I. I might be prepared to die for my country at some later date, but not as a virgin. Unbedded, I would be very choosy about the manner of my going into that dark night.

First, however, was the little matter of enlistment. Having completed the COTC aircrew course, I took my flying colours down to the RCAF recruiting centre, there to offer my A-1 body to the junior service. I had already previewed in the bathroom mirror how I would look with a white silk scarf draped rakishly around the neck I was about to stick out for king and country.

"Sorry, we don't need any more pilots," the recruiting

officer told me, not looking a bit sorry. In fact, my first and lasting impression of him was that he didn't have a sorry bone in his body. "With your math and map-reading training, you'll be taking the navigator's course."

"No, I won't," I said. I was familiar with the navigator's role as part of a bomber aircrew. He sat sideways in the cabin, poring over maps and drawing straight lines while the plane was being perforated by unfriendly missives from Messerschmitt fighters or enemy ack-ack. Instead of being a knight of the air, I would be part of the horse's assignation. Also, as a person who knew his potential for experiencing violent motion sickness in a variety of vehicles—father's car, trains, boats, office elevators, Ferris wheels—I could see myself trying to sort out a bombing target from a vomited raisin. Only when I was the one behind the wheel, managing the motion, did I also control the ejection seat of my breakfast. Determined to emulate my cousin, the Mad Mickey, I had not only my heart but my stomach set on serving as a pilot, preferably a fighter pilot. "I'm enlisting as a pilot," I told the recruiting officer with a finality that surprised even me.

He did not take kindly to my demurral. On the contrary, his face took on the same flushed exasperation as that of the Nelson school principal when he was doing his level best to reduce the palm of my hand to hamburger.

"If you're enlisting as air crew," he snarled, "you'll be assigned where you're needed—and it won't be as a pilot."

"Then I'll enlist as ground crew," I replied, thinking to pull his bluff. It didn't pull anything. He attacked the enlistment form with his pen.

"General Duties," he snapped, as though this were a particularly degenerative disease. "You're enlisted for General Duties. Report on Friday. Next!"

I had no idea what General Duties entailed. I suspected that I was not going to be partaking of the duties of a general. But just how far down the food chain the classification placed me did not become clear until I completed the enlistment procedure later in the presence of a corporal.

"It means you got no trade," he explained, glancing at me as though surprised to see a common labourer with such lily-white hands. "No trade, no trade's pay. Lowest of the low, Mac," he said with the relish of a Clerk, Grade 3, finding something beneath him in His Majesty's pecking order. "You need any help readin' that form?"

"Thanks. I think I can struggle through it." In a few minutes I was back to him with the form. "About this item 'Religion.' I don't subscribe to any orthodox religion. Shall I just leave it blank?"

"Nope." The corporal was very firm with his answer. "You got to have a religion to enlist in the air force."

So that I could reach up and touch the face of God? "I'm an agnostic."

A massive frown swept over his honest Canadian face. "Is that one of them Greek religions?"

"I'm afraid not. It means I don't belong to *any* church." Being something of a fanatic about my disbelief, I was prepared to go to the wall on this issue.

So, obviously, was the corporal, who growled, "Then you can't join the air force. We got to know your religion so we can put it on your dog tags. Otherwise they don't know how to bury you."

This solicitude about the sponsorship of my funeral service before I had even drawn my uniform failed to touch me as a valid expression of caring. "What happens," I said, "if I refuse to admit to a religion when I try to enlist in Canada's armed forces?"

"They'll draft you as a zombie." He nodded, knowing a clincher when he spoke one.

I could have pursued the philosophical debate about why the conscript was spared the need to wear a denominational dog tag. Presumably no one expected the zombie to be killed in action, and if he had a fatal accident, the body could be picked up by the SPCA.

"Okay," I conceded. "So what is the most popular religion among your recruits?"

The corporal squinted, clearly stressed by the need to think. "United Church."

"Fine. Put me down as United Church."

He hesitated, staring at me as though I might recently have come up through a manhole in a blast of flame and brimstone.

He thrust the form at me. "*You* write it." He was having no part of this pact with the Devil.

I did so, and became one of the fastest converts in the history of Christianity. I despised myself for compromising my intellectual integrity, only slightly consoled by the truism that the first casualty of war is truth. As for the dog tags— the one made to float if I bought it in the drink, the other to survive my being incinerated—the first thing I did after drawing my uniform was to toss them into a litter bin. If I fell in an aerial dogfight, they could inter me as the Unknown Religionist.

This baptismal immersion in the pool of recruits heightened my conviction that I was not the ideal type to go to war, as defined by the movies. I was neither the green kid scared out of his issue underwear, nor the laconic veteran, nor the wisecracking Jew, nor the black man smouldering from racial prejudice, nor the sadistic noncom. I had been cast in a war film for which no part for me had been writ-

Sergeant Erk, c. 1943. The ears alone would get me airborne.

ten. I was an extra, taken off the street. No audience is going to become emotionally involved with a character who regards the Nazis' attempt to conquer the world as a confounded nuisance. I would be killed off in the first reel. Ingloriously. Probably the first Canadian airman to die from German measles.

The departure date to Toronto No. 1 Manning Depot was

November 13, 1942. The leave-taking at Vancouver's Canadian Pacific Railway station—that great, echoing hall of farewells—was strictly a family affair, just Mom, Pop, and me. Other recruits were being seen off by sizable assemblies of friends and relatives. I had mustered the bare minimum of personnel to mourn my passing on to Toronto. And my father looked less grieved than relieved to see me finally saving the family from the disgrace of my receiving a white feather in the mail. We both knew that plenty of young Canadians—especially in Quebec and/or working in the shipyards—were qualified to draw enough white feathers to make a complete chicken. But as an old soldier and president of the Point Grey Branch of the Canadian Legion, my father was bound to feel uncomfortable until I was in uniform as a volunteer, and with at least some prospect of getting in harm's way.

My mother appeared less gratified. Her Italian, French and Irish bloodlines were, I thought, enjoying the drama of the situation, but she had been in Canada long enough to respect the inappropriateness of public display of emotion. The strain of inhibition from crying made her look more miserable than ever. I was genuinely afraid that at the last moment she would give way and plunge us into the cinematic cliché of her running tearfully beside the departing railway coaches, while I leaned out the window, smiling through a stiff upper lip.

Luckily friends and relatives were not allowed on the platform. And after a delay that exhausted all the relevant topics of conversation, and reduced us to such feeble remarks as "It's a nice day for a trip through the Rockies," we heroes were herded into our coaches, where I found my seat in the sleeping car. There, insulated from other recruits by the privacy of my thoughts—as were they from me—I watched the backsides of the waterfront warehouses ambling by, their windows mooning me at this critical moment in my life. How uncaring of the only city I had ever known to let me leave her harbour like this without so much as a tidal wave!

I had been assigned to an upper berth. Because I was an airman? Hard to say. Also hard to undress. I envied the veterans of this exercise, service people in uniform returning east from leave on the coast. They seemed more agile and more enterprising in their berth control, especially the busty sergeant of the Women's Army Corps whom I glimpsed— peeking through my curtain—as she chinned herself into the upper berth opposite. That she had joined someone already resident became audible by giggles that graduated into groans that disturbed me as being too basic to be blamed on the hard mattress. If this was close-order drill, I had much to learn. And with the train's wheels clucking, "Wickedly WAC...wickedly WAC," I sank into the slumber of the immaculately innocent.

Chapter 9

The Taking of Toronto

For four days and three nights I got a good look at the country I was supposed to be defending. There seemed to be an awful lot of it. Quite a responsibility. The Rockies alone were more than I'd care to try to hold without help. As my Troy, I'd choose the small Prairie town. No chance of the enemy's sneaking a wooden horse past *those* folk behind their stout redoubt of grain elevator. "The Breadbasket of the Empire." It was called such then, and I was privileged to enjoy an expenses-paid tour of the emperor's midriff. My personal discovery of all that pink space that my school atlas said was Canada—*bump!*— ended, with my train's halting in Toronto's Union Station.

We airmen recruits were off-loaded into the back of an open truck. No formal ceremony of welcome. No band, no crowd of pretty girls pressing flowers into our hands and kissing us with reckless abandon. Too soon, maybe. Instead we were brusquely herded into a rude vehicle of the kind that I associated with delivery of perishable fruit. Along with a half-dozen other apprehensive produce, I watched the Toronto waterfront fail to excite me as the truck delivered us to the Canadian National Exhibition grounds, where we debarked and were urged to enter one of the livestock barns. Since I was not a country boy, the homely aroma of my new home was less familiar to me than to those of my company with a rural background of sleeping with the cows. For *my* nose it meant sneezing, big-time. Already my schnoz was registering a violation of the Geneva Convention on the rules of war: airborne particles of bull shit.

The Sheep Pen. That was my domicile. Where I was assigned to an upper bunk—always an upper, never a bride—in this vast dormitory of hundreds of double-tiered cots, a reminder of home if home happened to be Kingston Penitentiary. Drawing my bedding, I was appalled to see that the latrine was a prolonged rank of johns marching as to war. Not a modest door in the squadron. The RCAF was ensuring that we comrades in arms had surrendered privacy. My viscera clamped shut immediately. Luckily they had already learned at logging camp how to go six weeks without a bowel movement. I just had another chance to confirm my entry in *The Guinness Book of Records*. (Only recently have X-rays for a barium enema revealed that I have what is called "a tortuous bowel," i.e., a few extra cloverleafs added to the freeway. A souvenir of Toronto.)

Worse horror awaited me—the Haircut. On the train east I had seen servicemen pointing at my hair and chortling. I thought that it was because I had slept in it. My hair was as important to me then as hair is to young men today. My

The staff of Wings, *tarted up by artist W. Coucill, Ottawa, 1944. (UBC)*

head was into the Samson Complex, evidenced by the thick, curly locks that my mother had nurtured to draw attention away from my ears.

"Everybody," ordered the NCO Sheep Pen, "go get a haircut."

"Pardon me, sir," I said. "I had a haircut just before I left Vancouver."

He smiled sweetly. "Congratulations. You've won another one."

I joined the queue at the shearing station. The recruit ahead of me went in, and a few minutes later a chap came out.

"You can go in now," he muttered.

I shook my head. "Another fellow went in ahead of me."

"That was me," he said ruefully.

My hair stood on end, a sort of farewell appearance. "What happened to your hair?"

He shrugged. "They said I wouldn't be needing it any more."

"Next!"

I went to the chair, glancing around, half expecting to see old hags knitting as they watched each execution.

"Sit down, sit down." The barber looked much like any other barber, except for the string of scalps hanging from his belt. He was quite bald. As I eased myself into the chair, he murmured, "My, you certainly had nice hair, didn't you?"

"*Had* nice hair?" I croaked.

"Sorry." He was jacking me into range of his clippers. "Just anticipating. Do you want to fasten your seat belt? We may hit some turbulence." He laughed, the clippers whined and the fiend was loose upon my hirsute pride and joy.

A few minutes later he swivelled me around, and I opened my eyes. The head I saw in the mirror wrenched a groan from my vitals. It had a brow crowned by a thick shock of skull.

"Will there be anything else?" he asked.

I shook the remains of my head. "No, I'll burn the eyebrows off myself."

"That will be two bits, please."

I gave him the money. No tip. I paused at the door. "Could I have a lock of my hair," I asked, "to remember myself by?"

I was given little time to get sentimental about being depilated. Other medical procedures quickly had me on parade in my undershorts. The first of these—called "short-arm inspection" by those of my fellow recruits worldly enough to be casual about the indignity—required me to stand in a long queue of the unclad to be scrutinized by a doctor whose eyes never rose above the waist. Somewhere behind me in the line a wiseacre was whispering, "I hear that yesterday a guy, when he gets to the doctor, gets a hard-on. So he grins and says, 'Hey, Doc, he likes you!' They put him on charge."

I could manage only a thin smile. I didn't know whether to laugh or moo at this cattle call for meat inspection. In any event, the obviously willie-weary doctor waved me through without cutting anything off. A mercy.

We were propelled along the disassembly line to a pair of doctors giving inoculation shots. Smallpox. Tetanus. Typhus. The whole charming gamut of plagues was mine to avoid. This, we were told, was why we were not allowed to leave the manning depot for two weeks. They didn't want us to have a bad reaction in the middle of Yonge Street and frighten the horses. We were reassured by a doctor who addressed the queue in a loud voice: "If you feel faint, put your head between your legs!"

First it's shaved, then my head between my legs for an indefinite period. Bad day for the loaf. I hadn't felt faint until the doctor mentioned it. Now I was teetering while still some distance from the pair of doctors wielding needles with the brisk efficiency of Singer sewing machines. I closed my eyes and thought hard about the sexism of swooning. Ladies can faint away gracefully, hand to brow, subsiding to the ground like the slow-motion film of a building demolition, poised long enough for a gentleman with any reflexes at all to catch the damsel in his arms. But a guy—the trooper on parade—drops like a stone. No time to put his head between his legs. Who says it's a man's world?

On reaching the two doctors I found that I had just

enough arms to accommodate all the needles. I studied the ceiling during the perforation until one especially prolonged stab made me look down. The doctor was holding a needle full of scary fluid.

"You're not going to inject that stuff into me, are you?" I asked hoarsely.

"No," he said. "I just took it out. It's your blood."

"Oh, good," I said, and I went to a bench and put my head between my legs.

To make a long day interminable, I was then directed to Stores to draw my uniform. No one, not even Salvador Dali, could have drawn the uniform Stores gave me. The clerks were all getting even for years of civilian life under the credo "the customer is always right." They manned a sort of sartorial assembly line, beginning with the basic chassis of long underwear, which I tried to wave off.

"No thanks. Never touch the stuff."

The clerk was not amused. "What size underwear d'ya take?"

Having just lost blood, my hair and my dignity, I was feeling light-headed. "Isn't that a rather personal question? After all, we hardly know each other."

"What *size*?"

I wet my dry lips. "It's either a thirty-eight, or a seven and three-eighths."

He plunked down two suits of long underwear, evidently expecting me to pick them up unassisted.

"Don't you have something lighter," I asked, "like a three-ply? A little more subtle in the seat?"

"Whaddya expect for free—venetian blinds?"

Jostled from behind, I packed away my long underwear to the next clerk.

"What size hat d'ya wear?"

"It's either a thirty-eight," I said, "or a seven and three-eighths."

He handed me something that looked like a tea cozy with a hangover.

"What's this?"

"That's your winter cap. The flaps keep you warm when it gets cold."

"That's what they said about the long underwear."

I was being sifted into a pair of trousers. They proved to be too big in the shoulders. The clerk gave me a size smaller, saying, "Don't worry. You'll gain fifteen pounds before you've been in the air force a month."

Nodding numbly, I stepped into the arms of a greatcoat held out for me or whomever was next. The greatcoat grabbed me under the arms, which hung out like a scarecrow. I was as snug as a bug in a mangle.

"Don't worry," advised the dispenser. "You'll lose fifteen pounds before you've been in the air force a month."

That night I put my two pairs of long underwear under my pillow and made a wish before dropping into a profound insomnia. But they were still there in the morning.

A few days later they let us out—for a route march. I would have chosen the route back home to Vancouver, but the NCO of our platoon didn't consult me. We clomped out of the CNE grounds in our nondesigner uniforms, and the first sight I saw, atop a building, was the huge sign: Tip Top Tailors.

Surely even the Marquis de Sade himself would have gasped at this cruelty: a sky-high reminder that I might never again wear a suit fit for other than a circus clown.

However, the winter-cap flaps quickly proved practical for a West Coaster being marched past Sunnyside Beach, with a refrigerant December wind blowing off Lake Ontario. My thinned blood could never have coped alone. A Vancouverite transferred to Toronto should be brought east in stages, across the Prairies, like a diver returning to the surface, so that his or her body has a treatable case of hypothermia.

However, the deep freeze cost me no parts of importance. It was a parade *inside* the bull shithouse that put me in jeopardy. Our squad was marched to a Sunday church service. Compulsory. I had no chance to point out to the commanding officer that my membership in the United Church was in name only, that I held my agnosticism sacred, et cetera. After the service, groups of us were ushered into the presence of the Protestant padre for a friendly chat. The padre told us, eyes twinkling, that it was theologically okay for us to utter obscenities—"fuck" and other manly sounds—but we must shun profanity.

"Never take the Lord's name in vain," he said.

Jesus, I thought, what kind of brainwashing is this? This smiley cleric-in-uniform is trying to tell me that when my plane is afire and spinning out of control I must scream, "Jiminy crickets!" Or, if *really* stressed, "Holy cow!"

In vain was the only way I normally took the Lord's name. Whereas I never used the f-word because it violated the awful mystery of sex. I left the padre's chummy briefing abristle with the rage of the intellectually righteous. Indeed, I was so incensed that on the following Sunday I went AWOL from the church parade, sneaking away to sit alone in the bleachers of the deserted cattle-judging arena. I was not missed, by God or man. But I thought I heard a cheer from T.H. Huxley.

Equally alone, I was set to sweeping the same cavernous ring, while other recruits had interviews to prepare them for their air- or ground-crew courses. No. 1 Manning Depot apparently didn't know what to do with me. I was not asked for suggestions. All I knew, as I swept livestock lint, was that I was now an aircraftsman, second class—an "erk." My orders were "If it moves, salute it. If it doesn't, paint it."

In what was clearly a desperation move, the Allied Forces posted me to Ottawa, the catch basin for the fundamentally useless. I found myself snorting ice crystals at Rockcliffe air station on what I came to think of as the lunatic fringe of the capital. The barracks were spaced so far apart that anyone lacking Inuit blood would be frozen in his tracks in transit, becoming a piece of statuary to supplement the cenotaph near Parliament Hill. In the early-January, subzero temperatures, my progress consisted of panic-stricken stumblings into buildings where I had no business to be—officers' mess...Women's Division barracks...huts with Explosives! Positively No Admittance! Outta my way, door. I'm not going on the national honour roll as a fudgsicle.

On the tenuous strength of my writing comedy, I was assigned to beef up the company of service personnel, of both sexes, mustered to produce *The Air Force Show*. Interservice rivalry to entertain the troops had been sharpened by the success of *The Army Show*. That show's stars— Johnny Wayne and Frank Shuster—were having a banner war. The navy was also making waves onstage. Someone at RCAF HQ believed that the honour of the junior service was at stake, and was hurling me into the breach.

I wrote little of the show. Mostly I just helped to warm the theatre by sitting in the front row with the director and watching Georgette, one of our WDs turned chorus girl, do things with her hips that couldn't fail to get an entire squadron airborne, or at least the part that mattered. Much as I had lollygagged over the showgirls of the West Coast, the Québécois women presented something ultrafeminine, a difference that hinted that a French kiss was something more than what Charles de Gaulle did when bestowing a medal.

Before I could establish a beachhead on Georgette, however, I was posted to Calgary—Public Relations, No. 4 Training Command HQ. It was even colder in Calgary than it had been in Ottawa. Was this how the air force was trying to get rid of me? By posting me to colder and colder climes until I was found frozen in a snowdrift, still clutching my portable, but with no dog tags to identify me?

Meanwhile I got a room of my own in a friendly boardinghouse within easy walking distance from the Hudson's Bay Company store in midtown Calgary. That was where No. 4 Command HQ was located: on the top floor of The Bay. At last I was getting off the ground, in the elevator to the sixth floor. The elevator moved too slowly to activate my motion sickness, but it was unsettling to share it with civilian shoppers as the female operator reeled off the merchandise to be found on each floor: "Ladies' lingerie...baby wear...sewing needs..." As an exhortation to victory, it wasn't quite in the same class as Henry the V's "Once more unto the breach, dear friends..." I felt somewhat marked down, as a warrior, when I stepped out of the elevator at the HQ floor.

My boss in the PR section was Flying Officer Jack Coldwell, son of M.J. Coldwell, one of the founders of the Co-operative Commonwealth Federation, which later became the New Democratic Party. Jack, an earnest, bespectacled and modest product of Prairie socialism, and a journalist, was as out of place in a capitalist war as I was. He issued orders apologetically; I received them with compassion. Neither of us believed that God was necessarily on the side of the Allies, the creator being morally inscrutable and none too easy to spot in a uniform.

The Command HQ was organizing a half-hour radio variety program in conjunction with Calgary station CFAC, utilizing the personnel on the dozens of RCAF units scattered across the Great Plains—people who on Civvy Street had been singers, musicians, comedians, any talent, proven or potential. Because of my experience with scripting *Stag Party*, I was designated to write the continuity and sketches for the program, as well as act as producer. The rest of the production staff consisted of Sergeant Harry Cluff, a tubby, semipro singer and comic, who would MC the show. The radio station provided a technician who arrived the day of the broadcast, took a few sound levels, hooked us into a line that hummed pitch as only a Prairie power line can hum, and—ta-dah!—show time! *Command Performance*, it was called.

All I had to do each week was travel to a different air force unit—High River, Edmonton, North Battleford, Moose Jaw, Lethbridge, any converted haystack—where the British Commonwealth Air Training Plan was processing the 131,553 graduated by the end of the war. At each unit Sergeant Cluff and I auditioned its potential performers. (We never had the heart to reject even the most morale-weakening tenor, especially if he outranked us.) I then wrote the script, timed the show and got us off the air smartly in twenty-nine minutes and forty seconds to the station band's spirited, if slightly uncoordinated, rendition of "The Air Force March."

From sweeping out the cow barn, this acey-deucey erk was suddenly head honcho, giving orders to sergeant fiddle players, flying officers coming out of the closet as Swiss yodellers, even the occasional squadron leader who fancied himself as another George Formby. Hey, this was fun. I had nothing against the war as long as I could be in charge. But sometimes I had a spot of bother when pulling rank. I had nothing on my sleeve except dandruff. I asked Jack, "Please, could you get me some stripes to go with my whistle?"

"I think that can be arranged," he replied, smiling. What a sweetheart.

A few days later my almost-new uniform was sporting three brand-new stripes. Acting Sergeant Unpaid, I now was. Which meant that I was working very long hours for the minimum wage. That was okay with me. I hadn't gone to war to make a killing.

But my expedited promotion did not sit well with other HQ NCOs, some of whom had spent years in the Permanent Force to earn even a corporal's chevron. Our warrant officer glared at me as though I must have slept my way to favour. I think he would have commented had he not lived in dread that the following week I would turn up wearing the scrambled-eggs cap of an air marshal.

Once, he did manage to cough up a bitter pill: "How come you're not in aircrew?"

"Motion sickness," I said, beaming. "You're looking at Puke City. Tossing my bickies in every conveyance since the baby carriage. Shall probably throw up in my hearse. Famous last whoops, eh?"

The warrant officer didn't take it well. I think he clung to the hope that, having run out of other bombs, the air force would forcibly transport me over Berlin to barf on Hitler's bunker.

Actually it was Canada's grain farms that bore the brunt. The need to hustle *Command Performance* weekly from training unit to training unit brought me, for the first time, into intimate contact with aircraft. I had to climb into planes that took leave of the ground. The worst kind. Sergeant Cluff and I had to hitch rides on any training craft headed in the general direction of our next broadcast site. For each takeoff I was sifted summarily into a parachute. No one showed me how to use it. After I had vomited in their plane a few times, pilots became even more perfunctory about providing for my survival in the event that I was thrown out of the aircraft.

These dawn patrols—for some reason that escaped me, the air force was infatuated with getting up with the lark—gave me an opportunity to become airsick in a wide variety of planes. Because Cluff was portly, the pilots never tried to squeeze us both into a rear seat of a Harvard trainer. But thanks to larger crates such as the Anson, I had ample room, and a convenient hole in the floor, to blitz all of Alberta and parts of Saskatchewan. (Later in my service career, assaulting the Pacific Ocean from a Canso flying boat, I extended my range to an upchuck into the salt chuck.)

My normal flight position, namely bent over a bag, gave me little occasion to reach up and touch the face of God, who was probably grimacing with the rest of the crew. At that time motion sickness was regarded as a sissy condition, like homosexuality. Real men don't "frow up"—that was the prevailing belief. I tried to tell other crew members that I would be fine, no problem, if they let me fly the plane on the strength of my holding a valid driver's licence. But there were no takers, and I was left to welter in shame. It was only years later that medical science at last provided an effective drug to counter the motion sickness caused by fluid sloshing about in the canals of the inner ear. Meantime I was *mal de merde.*

Chapter 10

Ottawa, Graveyard of Humorists

On the plus side, *Command Performance* proved to be no emetic. Our live audiences of station personnel laughed, cheered, applauded loyal support of their comrades-on-air. Our rating with radio listeners was equally gratifying. Among the talent discovered at our mike was a toothsome WD dental assistant whose Betty Boop imitation stopped the show. Her delivery of my lines, combined with *her* lines, earned her a regular spot on the show. Yet, as with all my wartime romances, the relationship was not sexually consummated. I had a mental block about the rightness of copulating with a woman—especially a woman in uniform—when I had not gone all the way to the scene of battle. It was all very well for an airman overseas in bomb-blasted Britain to live for the moment, but unless I was bayonetted by a clarinet, my life was not yet in real peril. And somehow that gave intercourse the aspect of a dishonourable discharge. This was a tragedy, since sex was about the only kind of transport in which I didn't get nauseated.

Command Performance having run its allotted thirteen weeks, the air force had to find me something else to do. I briefly considered asking for a transfer to another service, where I might see more active service and put paid to that fascist virginity, the dictator I had to sleep with. But *which* service? The navy? Not unless it gave up its dependency on ocean. The army? Fresh in my mind was the ghastly bungle of Dieppe, where most of the Canadian troops in the landing craft were violently ill before they even hit the beach, there to be cut down by German machine guns and mortar fire. Somehow khaki wasn't my colour. After all, sexual freedom wasn't *everything*. If the Nazi panzer divisions were prepared to meet me halfway, say, on the solid ground of Nova Scotia, I would give a good account of myself. Otherwise Heaven could wait.

This soul-searching was called off by my being posted back to Ottawa. I regretted leaving Calgary, a high-spirited filly of a town, whose clear, burbling Bow River and golden poplars brightened the spirit. I was also just getting to know Ida, the redheaded waitress in a restaurant where I ate all my meals. All that tipping down the drain.

Now I was off to Ottawa, a posting dreaded by every non-commissioned airman, soldier and sailor. Reason: the city was the HQ for the chiefs of staff and their multitude of officers. Ottawa had more brass than a gong factory which, in fact, it was, "gong" being service vulgate for "medal." All that braid rampant on the street meant that we lower ranks had to salute so often that veterans of the Ottawa front could be identified by their cauliflower right ears, disfigured by being incessantly struck by outstretched hands, and by their impacted fingers, buckled in collision with the sides of their heads.

On arrival in the capital I had to locate the downtown office of *Wings* magazine, the air force periodical to which I had been assigned as a staff writer. Using my COTC training in map reading, I got hopelessly lost. I stopped an elderly gentleman to ask, "Can you tell me where I might find *Wings?*"

He peered at my airman's uniform and wheezed, "Jeez, son, you'll need the whole plane."

I found the address I sought and mounted a well-worn flight of stairs in a building that had the musty air of having been around since John A. Macdonald. The steps squeaked a vote of no-confidence in the structure. On the second floor a door bearing the temporary, handwritten sign *Wings* beckoned me into what, I learned later, was an ancient medical facility abandoned by the federal government, probably because it was condemned by Florence Nightingale. One of the two large rooms still bore a fading rubric: Urinalysis. The whole place had a certain air about it that encouraged the opening of windows, summer and winter.

I introduced myself to the editor of *Wings*. This was Flight Lieutenant Gerald Anglin, an ebullient, bespectacled product of eastern journalism, destined to become editor of *Maclean's* and other national voices. I also met his subeditor, Sergeant Ed Hayes, who went on to a distinguished career with the *Kitchener-Waterloo Record*. At that moment, however, we were all square pegs trying to squirm into the round hole of the air force rondel.

Before setting up my portable in the urinalysis room—where I could expect a minimum of interruption by anyone with a nose—I was given time to find lodging in a rooming house on Rideau Street. The lady awarded me the attic penthouse, up one of those claustrophobically narrow flights of twisty stairs that are a specialty of old houses in Upper Canada. The first night there I was shaken from my bed when the building shuddered violently as if it had been bombed.

Oh, God, I thought. One of Hitler's battleships has made it up the Rideau Canal. I stumbled down three flights of stairs to join the other nightshirted residents huddled outside.

"It's an earthquake," someone said.

Unbelievable, I thought. I've travelled 2,800 miles from the most earthquake-prone region of Canada—the West Coast—only to experience being in a blender, here in Ottawa, where nothing is supposed to move without royal assent.

Now, as they say, nervous in the service, I applied myself to my duties as a *Wings* writer. One of these was to provide a second opinion for our editorial board which, for each month's issue, meticulously studied photos. The photos were not aerials of German airfields but glossy pinups of Hollywood actresses, distributed by the studios as part of the Allied war effort. If ever a small group of airmen showed devotion beyond the call of duty, it was in making the critical decision: Betty Grable smiling winsomely over her shoulder in her adhesive one-piece swimsuit...or Gene Tierney, whose black-lace lingerie was locked in a losing battle with her bosom...or leggy Ann Miller, her Texas-bred stems soaring to heights where man had never gone before? On our collective judgement depended the morale-supporting fantasies of tens of thousands of airmen. The full-page photo would be hidden inside lockers, under untold numbers of bunks, if not actually taped to a cockpit instrument panel.

Yes, this exercise was 100 percent sexist. To my knowledge, *Wings* never did publish the pinup of a half-naked male movie star. Our Women's Division had to serve their country with the beefcake severely rationed. I must share the guilt. To date, it has not necessitated my seeking counselling.

This was summer 1944. Better men than I had landed on the beaches of Normandy, and the final struggle to drive back the Hun had started. Air force recruiting was starting to taper off, with the Americans picking up the slack in the aerial war. So a new buddy of mine, Sergeant George Martin, and I decided to take advantage of the entry of the United States into the war by spending a weekend leave in New York City. Our uniform was passport enough to all manner of pleasure in the Big Apple, which had not yet contracted the scab that blighted it until recently. All that the Canadian service person needed was the price of train fare and a room at the New York YMCA. Grub was cheap at the Stage Door Canteen, and we had our choice of Broadway shows, gratis, simply by applying at the special armed-forces ticket agency.

Greedy for theatre, George and I grabbed tickets for a matinee, after which we dashed back to get ducats for an evening stage play or musical. We gorged ourselves enough to attract the interest of one of the volunteer ticket issuers, a very attractive brunette lady of median years, who invited us to spend the night at her estate on Long Island. Nothing loath, we caught the last train to the isle of the idle rich and were ushered into the presence of Mrs. Landmeyer, elegant in pink lounging pajamas. (We never met *Mr.* Landmeyer, or even sensed his presence.) Mrs. Landmeyer showed us personally to our room on the second floor of the mansion—definitely a cut above my Ottawa rooming house oubliette. Before undulating off to her own room, she indicated the direction of the bathroom at the end of the hall. *"Bonne nuit,"* she said in case we were Canadien.

I let George go to the bathroom first. He returned looking dazed, with more froth on his lips than normal from tooth-brushing.

"What happened?" I asked.

"You'll see," he said, sitting heavily on his twin bed.

Taking a firm grip on my own toothbrush and paste, I tip-toed down the hall to the bathroom. In so doing, I had to pass an open door. A *wide*-open door. I glanced into the room and was transfixed by the sight of Mrs. Landmeyer in a sheer black negligée, sitting at her vanity mirror and lan-guidly brushing her long black tresses. She smiled at me in her mirror, the smile segueing into a kissful pout. I dropped my toothbrush and paste, missed them on the first grab, straightened and grinned vacuously at my hostess.

"Just brushing my teeth," I explained, and bolted for the bathroom. Once there, I considered spending the night in the tub to avoid another confrontation. Eventually, with a towel over my head, I crept back down the hall. Wasted dis-cretion—Mrs. Landmeyer's door was now closed.

Back in my room, with George asleep, I had a guilt attack. I had let Canada down. This one I couldn't blame on motion sickness. I had failed to board an American craft that wasn't even moving. Why? Damn, I wasn't fit to pick up Churchill's cigar ash.

The next morning, when George and I descended to the drawing room, we found a British naval rating sprawled on the chaise longue, smugly smoking a cheroot.

"'Ad a good night, did we, lads?" he said, winking as he

blew a smoke ring. I felt better about being a coward. It was clear that Mrs. Landmeyer was collecting foreign servicemen the way other women collected fine china. And it was a lot more fun than selling Victory Bonds.

We never saw our acquisitive hostess again, and the butler sent us on our way with visible relief. Thus ended my only wartime encounter with the aggressive might of the United States.

Wings helped to restore some of my self-esteem by sending me on temporary duty to the West Coast, spewing on and writing articles from various operational units from Boundary Bay to the Queen Charlottes. I was braced for a posting overseas, a fearsome prospect, at that late stage of the war, because of the service mantra: "Last in, last out." Any Canadian airman sent to the United Kingdom in the last year of World War II could expect to be repatriated just in time for World War III. Some bods coveted the expenses-paid sight-seeing tour of Europe, despite some possible inconvenience east of the Rhine. Not I. I preferred to wait for the movie. Besides, I was forgetting what my M.A. thesis-in-progress was about, and my French irregular verbs had become downright unruly.

With the mothballing of *Wings*, I was posted to Montreal Public Relations, where I remained only long enough to learn that my academic French buttered no parsnips on St. Catherine Street. If there was one thing that offended a Québécois more than being addressed in English, it was listening to a *maudit Anglais* violating the patois of *la belle province*. Much as I admired the high style of Montreal's women—out west the way a woman walks indicates a desire to cover ground only—I was relieved to be transferred to the Trenton, Ontario, permanent air station on the thoroughly anglicized shore of Lake Ontario.

My job was to assist the public-relations officer with the press releases—mostly lists of repats—and to write speeches ghosted for the CO. Still classified as General Duties, I was at last doing one of the duties of a general. Or, in this case, a group captain. On several occasions I wrote the air vice marshal's speech to the station personnel, then stood on parade in the rain with the rest of the erks, hearing my own words burbling from the loudspeaker. A case of *déjà entendu*.

These duties left me with ample time to sabotage Canada's war effort with derisive articles for the station magazine, *Contact*, whose editor, a tautological treat named Sergeant Sargent, was also my roommate. A kindly bloke, he helped me recover from the shock of having to live in barracks for the first time, and within sight of the Women's Division huts.

To compensate for the loss of freedom, I was granted a crown to go with my stripes, and with it the right to be called "Flight"—the only volation without vomit that I enjoyed in three years of service.

Chapter 11

Back to Ivy-Covered Gall

I t was while on a forty-eight-hour leave in Toronto, riding in a streetcar, that I gazed in rapture at the headline on the front page of the newspaper dated August 9, 1945: "US Atom Bombs Hiroshima."

It was not my first impulse to question the political correctness of using a nuclear weapon that would bring the war to an end. Not really. No, my first thought was: Hurrah, I won't be needed to throw up on Tokyo.

My second thought was: How long before they let me get back to my war-torn M.A. thesis? The overseas vets, quite rightly, would be sprung first. It could be months before we marginal heroes were back on Civvy Street. As if to confirm my estimate, on my return to Trenton station, Stores issued me a new pair of boots. Those damn things were made to last for millennia. My hopes were shod.

Then, a blessed miracle. I was summoned to the orderly room and told by the adjutant that Dr. G.G. Sedgewick, head of the University of British Columbia English department, had requested my expedited release so that I might join his staff as an instructor and help to cope with the mass invasion of the campus by vets eager to cash in their Department of Veterans' Affairs educational benefits. Oh, frabjous day! No matter that I would be teaching English, though my own discipline was French. Hell, it was a multicultural country. G.G., desperate for bodies to put in front of the class, had remembered my newspaper columns as evidence of enough literacy to risk the blind leading the blind.

In September 1945 the campus of the University of British Columbia was happily suffering the growing pains of a suddenly enlarged enrollment. Grizzled veterans of the war mingled with downy-cheeked kids just out of high school. The vets were imbued with an almost unholy zeal to learn, learn, learn, especially since the government was paying for it. They had a new lease on life, fully furnished with questions they wanted answered. And this application rubbed off on the young so that the place reverberated with the impact of people hitting the books.

I was assigned to instruct two sections of English 206, a second-year course whose utilitarian purpose was to drum a modicum of communication skill into students pursuing a dog's breakfast of disciplines—physical education, commerce, nursing—and anyone else who in first year had wrestled with the language and lost in three quick falls. Having taken few English courses myself, as a minor to the French Honours program, I was ill-qualified to teach these unfortunates, just as my father had been in teaching accountancy on the strength of quartermastering after his discharge from

World War I. Like father, like son, in terms of a Mr. Chips whose effort to keep ahead of the class kept him hopping like a frog on a hot brick.

Since I had spent five years at university before resuming the M.A. program that could gain me employment as faculty, this cold plunge into professing taught me something I didn't want to know.

I was not a teacher.

The other English 206 instructors were able to recall their lecture notes year after year, simply by sucking a pipe, or cleaning their glasses a lot. I, in contrast, had to memorize an hour's lecture material every time I stepped in front of my class. This made for a lot of anxiety tinkles, as well as an underarm perspiration problem that required me to crimp my wing to the body when writing on the blackboard. I sweated it, literally, as a professor.

After a couple of winter terms of this repeated ordeal, I had to accept the bitter fact that I was mentally handicapped. The memory side of my brain, the jolly old data bank, was the size of a whistle pea. Because of some congenital screwup, I lacked the retention segment of grey cells that enabled other instructors to remember the names of their students years after teaching them. I forgot the name of a student minutes after he—and worse, she—had left my office. The more classes I taught, the greater the amount of embarrassment awaiting me when someone whose face was vaguely familiar greeted me on the street with "Hello, Mr. Nicol. You don't remember me?" That is no way to be well loved as a teacher. And I did want my students to love me, especially the leggy blonde who sat in the front row inviting conjugation. *Her* name I never forgot, but unfortunately I never met her again.

I have known one or two older professors afflicted with

the same memory curse. They solve the problem, rather badly, by never looking at another person. They avoid eye contact, stare straight ahead in public, or at the ground. You would swear that they were deep in ratiocination, but they don't fool me. They live in terror of being confronted by a former student, lover, dentist whose name is sailing on the River Lethe.

"Shy," or "reclusive," that's how normal people describe freaks like me who shrink from the crowded room. My worst nightmare is that of being trapped in a school gymnasium occupied by a class-reunion party. If I ever meet my Maker, I hope to God he's wearing a name tag.

Besides the strong inkling that I was not cut out for a career in cap and gown, I got an insight into the limitations on my creative writing. My "Mummery" columns again appearing in the *Ubyssey* (under the craven nom de plume "Jabez"), plus sketches for the national stage revue show *Spring Thaw* and pieces for magazines like *Saturday Night* and *Maclean's*, brought me to Earle Birney's attention. Birney was functioning as a UBC professor of English, but his poet's soul still belonged to the Muse. He organized a small writers' circle that met occasionally to read and discuss the work of each member. The author of "David" was, of course, the messiah around whom we apprentice apostles of Can Lit clustered, clutching our grubby manuscripts and—something I was never good at—exposing innermost feelings in verse or prose. Novelists Ernie Perrault and Bill McConnell were members, with poets like Phil Thomas and Hilda Halpin, and sometimes the awesome Ethel Wilson.

It soon became apparent to me that as a scribbler of light essays I was in way over my head without a life jacket. Usually sexual in theme, most of the poems read baffled me. Never mind the symbolism, I missed the gist. All of it. In discussions I sat like a toad full of shot. The one time I ventured to question the image in one of Phil Thomas's erotic poems, a line that went something like "... her legs moved languidly as butterfly's wings," the group stared at me as though I had only recently come down from the trees.

Birney, of course, never missed a sexual allusion in word or woman. Although we became friends, I never adapted to the *laissez-aller* lifestyle of this, probably Canada's finest poet. Genius grants licence. Those of us short on it, especially such as I who let a sense of moral responsibility get in the way of earned whoopee, deserve our fate as shaded lamps.

Earle and I both loved women, but in ways whose difference is illustrated by an incident one summer when I was a guest, with Birney and a married couple, at Einar Nielsen's cottage on Bowen Island. Einar, the island cabdriver and patron of the arts, enjoyed entertaining the literary icons who let their hair down at his rustic abode.

That afternoon I was helping Earle split shakes for the cottage roof. I spotted an open boat, out in the bay, graced by a couple of young women in skimpy swimsuits. I picked up the nearby binoculars for a closer look, upon which Earle remarked, "Just like a guy—always looking for something better when he's got a cottage full of cunt."

"Heh, heh," I said, yukking off my shock. Coming from a mouth that publicly spoke such sensitive verse, the coarse c-word made my guts cringe. We had a different regard for women. Case closed.

As for Ethel Wilson, I was more comfortable with that lady, though not much. A startlingly beautiful woman, Wilson had a bad leg, and spent her latter years in a wheelchair, mad as hell at what Fate had dealt her, yet writing the gracious novels that gave no hint of that monstrous imposition.

She was far too brave for me, as Birney was much too macho. I stuck to hitting on the badminton shuttle.

At a party that the Birneys held to honour the visiting Dylan Thomas, I pressed the great poet's sweaty palm, inhaled his booze-enhanced breath and realized that as a teetotaller I was disqualified from the divine madness.

Earle's *cénacle littéraire* impressed upon me that I have a deadweight literal mind. My consciousness cannot be raised without an industrial-strength jack. Although I did not know it at the time, this rationality would later disqualify me from understanding a whole decade of contemporary society: the Age of Aquarius. In 1947 Aquarius was, to me, just a drip. People bought newspapers for the well-written accounts of news and opinion, rather than to check their horoscope and winning lottery numbers. I was lucky enough to have a few good years before I was over thirty—too old to blow my mind, yet too young to be clinically senile.

The literal mind was however ideal for completing my M.A. thesis. The topic, "L'Idée de l'Europe," had been chosen for me by the head of the French department, Dr. David Owen Evans. He was a brilliant but moody Welshman, a closet socialist, by my reckoning. Evans was always pleasant to me, a palpable pleb in class, but when one of the socialite girls in his class failed to do her homework assignment, his wrath was terrible to behold. I made a point of wearing my bicycle clips to class to help substantiate my belonging to the proletariat.

I laboured like an academic navvy to build the M.A. thesis into a credible synthesis of French authors—all of them stultifyingly dull—presaging the union of Europe's nations. Now that the European Union is in the process of effacing the ancient frontiers, I wish I could remember something, *anything*, of what it took me so many hours to drudge through. My recall facility will have none of it. What it does remember with infinite melancholy is my sitting in my carrel in the library's stacks, seeing from my window the pretty coeds in their party frocks and their tux-clad escorts tootling into the student building for a prom, or a pep meet, or other social occasion that I couldn't afford in time or money. Having shown no aptitude whatever as a scholar, I seemed to be preparing myself for a career as a monk in a French abbey that made mediocre wine.

I was living at home again with my parents, who had moved to a different house in Point Grey, but I still found them. I paid $75 a month board, but I could tell that my absence during three years of war had not been altogether unbearable for my father. Since I was nearing thirty, he may have felt a twinge of remorse when Hirohito packed it in, releasing the son who snapped back into the family fold like a rubber ball to the paddle bat.

I brought home a sequence of dates to meet my parents. My father liked them all as potential daughters-in-law, sensing that he would not so much be losing a son as gaining a room. But my mother was picky. She wanted me to get serious about a sensible girl, probably wearing glasses and happy to wait on me hand and foot. Since neither my hand nor my foot was the appendage having first call on my being well served, it was difficult for the Nicols to achieve a consensus.

In 1947 Ryerson Press published my first hardcover book, *Twice Over Lightly*. It comprised a collection of pieces that had appeared in the *Vancouver News-Herald* and periodicals like the *British Columbia Digest*. Because of the enormous popularity of *Reader's Digest*, digest magazines proliferated in the 1940s, and it was a pretty poor writer of short articles who couldn't get himself digested somewhere. Also, people were still reading before the mid-century, television not yet having reared its ugly bunny ears. With three daily newspapers in Vancouver, writers such as Jack Scott, Pierre Berton and Bruce Hutchinson helped to create a literary medium from the froth estate.

The adventurous literary spirit of the time is indicated by the fact that the publisher of *Twice Over Lightly*, Ryerson Press, was the United Church's publishing house. Were they being grateful to me for my choosing the United Church as my faith rather than face conscription? Not likely. The Toronto publisher could smell a buck, not incense. But being bound into books by a publisher of hymnals did restrict my style of humour somewhat. If offered the kind of thing written today by the likes of Phyllis Diller and Dave Barry, the manager, an ex-minister, would have tossed his collar over his head in a fit of the vapours.

I couldn't get away with even a *single* entendre. Not only did the United Church not entertain the idea of ordaining homosexuals as ministers, but the mere mention of the word would cause a frisson that flaked the paint off the walls of the stern pile in downtown Toronto the Good.

Despite carrying this handicap weight of propriety, *Twice Over Lightly* did reasonably well in the Canadian humour stakes of 1947. A critic would be hard put to find in those burblings the influences of the authors, from François Villon to Jean Giraudoux, whose works were the grindstone hosting my nose during years of French courses. In those courses French humorists were rather thin on the ground. I envied Rabelais for his being able to write, in *Gargantua*, about giants urinating in hilarious volume. The nuggety aphorisms of Le Duc de la Rochefoucauld delighted me, his perversity striking a sympathetic chord with such gems as "What we pride ourselves on as strength of will may actually be feebleness of desire." Or "We all have the strength to endure the misfortunes of others." Touché!

Montaigne I still read as the paragon of personal essayists. It strikes one dumb with wonder the way he set out sparklers of wit and wisdom to illuminate the remaining dark places of the medieval European mind. He established the seniority of the essay genre, sired the family dating from Francis Bacon and still vigorous in the essays of my heroes, James Thurber and E.B. White. The *New Yorker*, then in its glory, was my scripture for the 1940s and 1950s. Robert Benchley and Canada's Stephen Leacock were proving that the world looks even funnier seen through a bottle. Humour's *âge d'or*.

Having at last marched across the stage of UBC's Auditorium to be lassoed with the blue-lined hood of the master of arts, I decided to combine the discovery of the Old World with the acquisition of a doctorate from the University of Paris. A degree from the Sorbonne would be a first-class ticket to professorial status. Dr. Nicol. I liked the sound of it. It was like the clink of coins into a piggy bank. And just as puerile, given that teaching had much the same effect on my stomach contents as flying through turbulence.

More practically, I still had enough credits from the DVA to fund a couple of years' living in Paris, unless I took a mistress with expensive tastes, such as eating. I had also squirrelled away money in the bank for years with a post office account opened in my teens, which I continued through service in the air force. My interest-bearing savings were one of the few things I was prepared to defend to the death. Like most other Canadians whose formative years were cribbed by the Great Depression, financial means have been my security blanket, and I have never tired of trying to make it king-size. *L'Avare* is the only Molière play I have never found really amusing. And I have always had a soft spot in my head for Volpone. I think that both gentlemen took a bum wrap in being identified as misers.

So, during all those years of French studies, nothing coming out of Montreal interested me as much as the Bank of. *Maria Chapdelaine* was all very fine, but for reading that gave me a real rush, nothing compared with the current balance in my B of M passbook. I count myself lucky, now, that student loans were not available in the 1930s and 1940s. Had the government purse been open I might have ignored Polonius's sound advice "Never a borrower nor a lender be" and laid the sleeve on alma mater. A dangerous precedent. Having accepted a loan once, I would have found it easy to buy a car "on time," take out a mortgage to purchase my house, borrow on my credit card, none of which I have ever done. Like other ancients, I now move incredulously through a society that takes it for granted that it has a right to things—a car, a house, a child—before it can afford them.

The Depression had taught me another hard lesson: Do not depend on other people for your self-reliance. That was why, when I packed my old suitcase for the voyage to Paris in the fall of 1948, I snuggled my air force "housewife"—a khaki cloth binder for needles, thread, wool and extra buttons—into one corner. The couturiers of la rue de la Paix would not be making a sou from me.

Out of respect for my motion sickness, I had taken care to book passage from New York City on the largest ship plying the Atlantic: the *Queen Elizabeth I.* This mighty vessel had conquered the seas as a troop ship, I knew, without losing a single soldier to the heaves. As steady a stance as John Bull's.

Wrong! We were barely out of New York harbour, while I was still waving to the Statue of Liberty, in fact, when I was obliged to descend verdantly to my bunk, not to see daylight—my steerage-class cabin being below the waterline—until the ship was nearing Cherbourg. Staggering up on deck, light-headed from five days on a diet of dry biscuits and water, I could not believe that what I was seeing was the approaching coast of France. The only coast I had ever seen before was Canada's West Coast, a profile of mountains roaring six thousands of feet or more into the sky. Europe was coming at me as a disadvantaged horizon. I had to take a steward's word for it: behind that thin lip of land lay a whole continent, with legitimate mountain ranges and quite adequate rivers. The Old World was simply worn down a little at the edges from the feet of centuries of invading armies traipsing back and forth across the English Channel.

French customs and immigration looked at the photo in my passport with some suspicion.

"I've been sick," I said, still hiccupping from the week's fasting and retching. "Normally I have flesh."

Now ravenously hungry, I was bundled onto the boat-train to Paris. "Food!" I cried piteously. "I need food!" I was handed a box lunch. It contained an orange, which I was too weak to peel, and *un sandwich*, a wafer with an attitude. This was to sustain me for the ten-hour ride. Maybe I had made a mistake, I thought, as I watched the bullet-pocked ramparts of Cherbourg crawl past, in not coming over earlier with the Canadian infantry. At least they ate well.

By the time—after midnight—that our engine hooted effeminately into the Gare du Nord, I was beginning to hallucinate. Luckily there was someone there to slap my face. Howard Rigney, another English instructor from UBC and a good friend despite his having scoffed up all the meals on the *QE*, assisted my detraining by pointing me in the direction of the exit. There, to my groggy horror, we and other North American students arriving on the train were greeted by a covey of young French students waving a banner that declared, Bienvenus à Paris! They insisted on helping us carry our bags to the nearest bistro, where they ordered brandies for everyone. No food. Just brandies. I had never before drunk brandy, or any other fortified wine, but it seemed ungracious not to accept the cordial, even though it accelerated the rate at which the square was revolving around me.

After we guests had paid for the brandies, most of the welcoming party disappeared. Only one remained to advise Howard and me and a couple of Americans that our destination, La Cité Universitaire, lay on the outskirts of Paris, that the Metro underground had stopped running for the night and that the few taxis—still blackout-headlighted with slits of yellow cats' eyes—were all *occupé*. The City of Light was dark and dormant.

We therefore trustingly followed our guide down empty and echoing streets to the black hulk of a flophouse that we later learned had been a brothel during the war, now abandoned by the residents. En route we were whistled at by a cluster of *belles de nuit* standing under a streetlight.

"Comme ils sont beaux!" ("Get a load of those hunks!") they cried.

I wasn't in the mood. What with malnutrition and cognac, my sexual response was nil. The two Americans, having sized up the lightless room in which squatted cots with no mattress, opted for the hookers. Any bed in a storm. But Howard and I, being Canadians, lay meekly down on the fakir's delight. I used my orange as a pillow and lay awake for the rest of the night, peering fitfully at a pile of sacking in the corner that from time to time uttered a low moan.

In the morning I ate my pillow and had a pee down a black hole in the floor, a chilling cascade to unknown depths that I feared would bring up the hounds of Hell, steaming with rage, to savage my private parts. I remember little of how Howard and I reached Cité Universitaire, except that my fainting on the Metro was prevented by the support of French folk crowded into the car on their way to work. Nothing could drop there except the value of the franc.

I have a vague recollection of meeting the manager of La Maison Canadienne, a blue-rinse matron named Madame, who assigned Howard and me to a single room on the second floor of this chaste embassy of Canadian education in France. There I fell on the bed and slept, the first unbroken slumber since leaving North America. Lafayette, we are here. Please do not disturb.

Chapter 12

La Vie de Bohunk

C ité Universitaire was, and I presume still is, a scattering of national residences for students of various countries enrolled in colleges in Paris. In a parklike setting flanking Boulevard Jourdan, which is part of the circular highway skirting the *portes*, or gates, to the city, the student houses were sufficiently remote from the Left Bank to attenuate any hankering for *la vie de bohème*, something that inhibited foreigners like myself might have brought into the country as part of their hormonal baggage.

I envied those of my colleagues who were affluent enough to afford to rent a picturesquely squalid garret close to the fabled Café de Flore and other resorts of the Hemingways and the Sartres. With Madame supplementing the beady-eyed male concierge, there was absolutely no way a resident of La

Maison Canadienne could get *une petite amie* up to his room, short of block and tackle from a window. Not only was the house noncoed, but the Québécois students were separated into a choicer wing than us *maudits Anglais*, as if the administration had been instructed to preserve the Two Solitudes except for sharing the john and the one house phone.

This arrangement guaranteed that I would be speaking little French. A pity, this, since my fluency in the spoken language was glacial. I didn't have it in the throat. "You have to roll your arse," a teacher once told me, but my arse refused to roll. Now the fellows cohabiting a downtown flat with a Parisienne coquette would return to Canada, and their wives, well prepared to teach French at the high school level, or even collegiate, if they had spent some time talking. It was enough to shake one's faith in clean living.

However, I had to speak French when I made my first visit to the Sorbonne in the academic heart of *la Rive Gauche*. Purpose: an interview with the professor who had drawn the short straw and was to supervise my doctoral thesis. The Sorbonne itself, architecturally, was a bit of a disappointment to me. I had envisioned it as a cozy cluster of cloisters, with monklike members of faculty strolling through sunny arcades to the soothing babble of fountains and philosophy. Instead I found cold stone. The stark building was unheated—the French were very formalized about turning on the heat no earlier than November 1 and turning it off, unnegotiably, on March 31. So, everyone was wearing his or her overcoat in class. I wished I had brought my air force winter cap, with the flaps to keep the ears from freezing. As it was, I had trouble making notes wearing mitts. I soon learned that body heat was a major factor in successful completion of a course of study at the Sorbonne.

I also had difficulty tracking down my assigned prof. On many of the office doors was affixed a small card advising that the resident would be unable to meet his students because he was on a sabbatical in Tahiti. When at last I cornered a faculty member who had the misfortune to be instructing for the term, he promptly dismissed my thesis subject—"Le Style de Jean Giraudoux." The plays of Giraudoux had enchanted me as the apotheosis of contemporary French stage comedy, and I was looking forward to at last working on a thesis subject that didn't leave me colder than yesterday's mashed potatoes.

"*Giraudoux,*" sneered my Sorbonne professor, "*c'est un artiste.*" He spoke the word as though being an artist were a rather dirty habit, like picking one's nose. He then tried to sell me on the idea of doing a doctoral thesis on the language of the kitchen from 1720 to 1810. I was to learn later that he had browbeaten another Canadian doctoral applicant into spending a year or two of his life documenting the language of the kitchen from 1650 to 1720. The professor was obviously building his own magnum opus, "The Language of the Kitchen," from the year dot to 1948. We would be paying tuition fees in order to shackle ourselves to a crashing bore of a task, slaves of this foxy pharaoh constructing the pyramid of his own reputation.

I balked. I hadn't travelled 8,000 miles in order to get immersed in vintage pots and pans. The language of the boudoir, yes. I could see a potential for interesting research in the bedroom. But the kitchen, no way. I told the professor that I would be registering my thesis as "Le Style de Giraudoux." From the dismissive manner with which he terminated the interview, I inferred that I could expect to see him again about the same time that pigs grew wings.

This was the beginning of a disillusionment with the

University of Paris that grew into downright disgust. The monks had become as exploitive as aluminum-siding salesmen. *Quel dommage!*

It took me a while to grasp what had been well known to generations of writers: Paris provides a wonderful education as long as you stay away from the colleges. In short, the city itself became my thesis. Walking, walking, walking its pavements, I learned Paris as she was three years after VE Day: a handsome, elegant *grande dame* with a chipped tooth. Her citizens didn't deserve her. I discovered that Paris is the opposite of Moose Jaw, Saskatchewan, where the town is not memorable but the people are lovely.

A product of Canada's rain forest, I had to live in Paris to learn to respect trees. The double rows of plane and chestnut trees bordering the *grands boulevards* gentled the architectural wonders, and added the values of seasonal change, the mix of sweet and melancholy that Edith Piaf was voicing with "La Vie en Rose."

To be handier to this heart of Paris, and incidentally to research my thesis, I more or less set up shop in the Bibliothèque Nationale, hard on la rue Richelieu. I spent more hours in its vast reading room than I did in the Sorbonne or La Maison Canadienne, neither of which provided a place to write except the WC. In time I developed the same affection for *la grande salle* that Bernard Shaw felt for the British Museum, as a Dubliner trying to establish himself in London without having to rent an office.

At first the national library fazed me because its main purpose seemed to be to deny people access to books. This was quite a change from the library of the University of British Columbia, where it was easy for senior students to gain admission to the stacks and pick up any book whose title caught their fancy. In the Bibliothèque Nationale, having survived the scrutiny of the uniformed concierge, and been assigned to a numbered desk among the silent, green-lamped rows, I had to submit a *chiffre* (call slip) to one of the librarians manning the parapet fronting the room. And if that person found it valid, he or she dropped it into a slot that fed it to God only knew how many gnomes toiling, like Quasimodos, in the nether regions of the fortress.

Eventually a uniformed and very elderly courier would totter along my aisle and deposit on my desk the book I had ordered. No tip. The whole process took on average a half hour, leaving me plenty of time to use my desk for extracurricular activity, which I happily did. It was on that discreet blotter that I began writing columns from abroad for the *Vancouver Province*, the first of the nearly 6,000 published over the next forty years. Each column—describing the French experience—earned me $10 Canadian, which at that time was worth almost $10 American, and the price of a week's restaurant meals on the black market.

Yet food was a problem for me in the Paris of 1949. Since I was neither pregnant nor a minor, my ration book entitled me to only a litre of milk a week. The milk was sold in bulk and was ladled into my bottle at the *laiterie*. In warm weather that meant it had to be drunk immediately, since La Maison had no fridge. This left me with six milkless days, a disaster for someone whose whole lifestyle at home was based on lactose in various forms—by the glass, in custard pies, bread puddings, white tea...To be deprived of my daily fix of moo juice shook my system with withdrawal symptoms. The drinking water being suspect—the Seine is an interesting shade of jade, but I wouldn't want to gargle it—I was forced to take wine with my meals. Wine was not totally unknown in western Canada in the 1940s, but was still something of an exotic in terms of alcoholic beverages.

Real men drank beer in what was called a "beer parlour," while the unreal imbibed rye by the mickey, usually carried into a nightclub in a brown paper bag and placed under the table in case the joint was raided. ("Mine? Oh, no, Officer, I never saw that crock before in my life!")

To see a bottle atop the table instead of beneath it took some getting used to, as did the taste of the stuff. The red *vin ordinaire*, of which I ordered a modest carafe, may have *looked* very much like the grape drink that was my favourite libation at the tennis club in Vancouver, but the effect was entirely different. It turned my humble cheese omelette—my staple diet in a city where all meats, however described on the menu, were likely to have once belonged to a horse—into something of an event. The visceral glow generated by a glass of wine at Le Coq d'Or clarified for me what the Frenchman means when he says, "A meal without wine is like a day without sunshine." The sun sure came out a lot more warmly than it had in Vancouver. The Paris sky was bluer, the Eiffel Tower more stately, the Champs Elysées more paradisal than any vista that Vancouver afforded on the strength of a vanilla milk shake.

But I had a problem with the more solid elements of bistro meals. Some of my fellow Canadian students, besides going all to hell with casual sex, plunged rapturously into a *carte du jour* that to my conservative West Coast eye was a minefield of offal. Frogs' legs were the least of my worries. Anyone can spot the underpinning of an amphibian on his plate. The meat pie in the restaurant window, the crust pierced by the head of a lark complete with feathers—*"Alouette, gentille alouette"*—warned me off all types of pastry. But I still had stomach-churning run-ins with dishes such as *ris de veau*, which I ordered under the impression it was veal with rice. When the waiter explained that what I had partly consumed was, in fact, a sweetbread, part of the calf's reproductive system, I gagged and croaked the one phrase I felt safe with: *"L'addition, s'il vous plaît."* I never fully accepted the Frenchman's earthy relish for the edible parts of anything that moved. I found that I was too squeamish to be a gourmet. I define the square meal.

In the matter of enjoying *human* flesh, however, I was much more in tune with Gallic verve. Even before I left Canada, I was smacking lickerish lips in anticipation of being in the burlesque theatre long exalted to the status of an international institution: the Folies Bergère. Josephine Baker, the black American idol of Paris, was pulling in the crowds at another house, but I was not interested in musical talent. My craving was for the spectacle of beautiful women naked but for a few feathers adorning their heads and a string of beads where it didn't matter. The raw pornography of Montmartre's *boîtes de nuit* and gynecological postcards held no appeal for me. I had dutifully admired the Venus de Milo at the Louvre, and now I would visit this other famous museum, the Folies, where the exhibits moved and breathed. Especially breathed.

It was, of course, a disappointment. For one thing, my cheap seat was so far from the stage that even with my twenty-twenty vision I couldn't be sure that the *première nue* was not, in fact, a *premier nu*. The French, I found, have this lamentable way of neutralizing the visitor's prurient appetite by making nudity look perfectly natural. The *au naturel*. They even do it on their Riviera beaches. No wonder they are famous for their clothes designers. They have absolutely no regard for honest North American voyeurism.

Somewhat disillusioned, I thereafter concentrated on the more legitimate theatre of Paris. With a student's-price ticket I ranged the entire gamut, from the Roland Petit ballet to the raunchy Grand Guignol. Opera, the Comédie Française, I stood in the gods almost nightly for this feast. Sometimes I treated myself to a *strapontin*, a spring-hinged stool in the aisle of the theatre, working on the principle of a levitating toilet seat. The sitter's weight made the difference between stasis and being catapulted into the orchestra pit. I had left Vancouver weighing a well-padded 195 pounds, but on my Paris diet of bread and cheese I was losing the pounds fast, and when poised on a *strapontin* was ready to yell, "Geronimo!" as I was ejected into space. I was most comfortable when the act on the stage was acrobats. I could blend.

With the coming of springtime, I spent most of my lunch hours strolling in the magnificent parks of Paris. Bench sitting may not be as poetically stimulating as café-sipping the absinthe that traditionally lubricates genius, but it is easier on the pocketbook. I became a regular in the Luxembourg Gardens, wincing at the Fontaine de Medicis grotto of the two naked lovers entwined under the benign gaze of Eros. ("Hey, Eros, what am *I*—chopped liver?")

It was under the leafy canopy of the Tuileries that I had my first, and last, romantic encounter of my stay in Paris. A peerless June evening, it was, with summery folk gathered on deck chairs to enjoy a military band concert. I was cruising. I cruised a lot in Paris without picking up anything but dog doo. Dog doo, and the sidewalk *pissoir*, were two good, smelly reasons to cruise in the park, where *les chiens* were *interdict*. But girls were allowed. I had learned, to my dismay, that the French granted no middle ground for their daughters: either the girl was a whore, or she was so closely chaperoned by her family that a visiting foreigner had a better chance of picking up Notre-Dame. I had to hope I'd be adopted by some family that wasn't home much.

So, on this enchanted evening, with the *bassins* of the Tuileries Gardens ejaculating with a force that set the standard for a young man's fancy, I strolled among the concert audience. Miraculously I happened upon an empty chair beside a ravishing young woman wearing a long, lacy white frock that shimmered in the dusk, and a broad-brimmed white chapeau that completed her reproduction of a romantic Renoir. I eased into the chair, and she turned to give me a smile, a flash of spectacularly white teeth, framed by a face tanned to counterpoint her elbow-length white gloves and the white parasol folded in her lap.

For once I had the presence of mind to smile back. In previous such circumstances my wont, when unexpectedly smiled upon by a beautiful girl, was to hyperventilate. By the time I regained control of my pulmonary and circulatory systems, the magic moment had passed. But this time I caught the cue. I let my eyes speak the urgent message that I normally censored as too explicit for viewing in prime time. She dropped her gaze, as a nice girl will when hit by the horny butcher's, then quickly, as a nice girl will, let her eyes say, "Thank you. Now let's get verbal."

We chatted. Lugubriously, for me. To convey my meaning, I depended heavily on my elbow resting against hers. To clarify it further, I took her gloved hand in mine, whereupon all the churches in Paris rang out an inaudible carillon, and Joan of Arc, on her column's steed nearby, urged a silent *"Allez-y, mes enfants!"*

Wonder piled upon wonder: the relatives that Yvette was with melted away into the darkness to leave me alone with this diaphanous creature. The family trusted me! With their daughter! In the dark of the park! And I wasn't even wearing a maple leaf logo on my jacket!

We kissed in the moonlight, and when she said demurely

that she had to return to her hotel, I escorted her and drew a promise to meet me for breakfast at a bistro nearby.

I have no memory of how I passed the rest of that magical evening, But I was in my chair early at the bistro in bright morning sunshine when Yvette came to join me. When she sat down, I noticed something for the first time.

She was quite, quite black.

In the darkness of the Tuileries Gardens I had seen her skin tone as a tan that spoke volumes about her hormones. In daylight Yvette turned into a relatively terrestrial young woman from North Africa, visiting town. Before I could subdue racial qualms, she told me she would not be seeing me again because she was returning to her home in Algiers, where her father was the manager of the Gillette razor franchise. Aside from the hazard of seducing the daughter of a man with unlimited access to blue blades, I had to accept that we had met from two different worlds that were in rare alignment. I shook her beautifully snake-skinned hand in farewell—an aerobic exercise of the bittersweet.

This was as close as I came that year in Paris to having my confounded celibacy dismantled. The failure was one of the major shames of my youth. There was no excuse for not consummating such an idyllic romance. Had it been the University of Toronto that I was attending, and the evening concert was at Massey Hall, yes, then discretion would have been justified. But in Paris I blew it. It would not have surprised me if France now refused to renew my student's visa. They can sense these things.

Yet I was not sleeping alone.

About this time I became involved in what the annals record as L'Affaire des Punaises, or the Bedbug Affair. In one of my weekly letters home to my parents (who presciently saved them), I gave an account of this sordid slumber party.

Here it is edited for family viewing:

As you know, if you've been following my letters attentively, Rigney and I have recently been in more different bedrooms than Casanova in his heyday. The resemblance ends there, however, since Casanova had fun testing the springs, whereas Rigney and I were strictly DPs, victims of the militant *lebensraum* philosophy of a bunch of bedbugs. Originally we were in room 4. Then came Black Friday, the day I discovered that the bugs were enjoying my crunchy goodness and writing unsolicited testimonials for every bug in the Fourteenth District. Rigney and I were moved upstairs to room 30.

"You must have brought the bedbugs from Canada." This from Madame, the manager.

"We don't have bedbugs in Canada," I said. "All our bugs sleep outside."

Although officially in a state of denial, Madame quietly instructed Claude, the concierge/totum factotum, to treat my room with *la bombe*. Setting off *la bombe* required only slightly less preparation than that at the Alamogordo air base in New Mexico. All the residents in our wing of the building had to quit their rooms during the countdown and for several hours after the detonation of the device in my sealed chamber. Those residents thereafter looked at me as giving comfort to vermin, a pariah that should not be allowed abroad unless sealed in a container properly labelled Buggy.

When at last Rigney and I were permitted back

into our room, I slept uneasily with the residual fumes of cyanide or whatever *la bombe* had been loaded with. Thus I was awake early enough to observe a huge bedbug striding across my bed-sheet with the vigour of an insect not only immune to explosive pesticide but energized by it. Enraged, I tore my bed apart. I heaved the heavy wooden mattress frame onto its back on the floor and stared, incredulous, at the scene revealed in the corner of the frame.

There was a veritable colony of bedbugs. Big bedbugs, little bedbugs, pregnant female bedbugs, a great-grandpa bedbug that had probably been sucking human blood since the Third Empire. My body had been serving as a buffet for enough bedbugs to make Dracula look bush-league.

Claude, when summoned to examine the evidence that *la bombe* had served merely as an aperitif, muttered, *"Merde,"* and expunged the varmints with a couple of vicious swipes of a broom.

This was my lone encounter with bedbugs in France or elsewhere, but it left me emotionally scarred. Today, when introduced to someone who smiles slyly and says, "I know more about you than you think," I assume she has been told that I am the person who introduced the Canadian bedbug to Europe. Nor did my roomie, Rigney, fully recover from our being bombed. A quiet, sensitive soul from Ontario, he seemed to stop breathing every time I looked closely at something. A ladybug almost finished him. With only one desk in Room 4, Rigney and I had to take turns, with one man writing on his bed. When I got eraser crumbs on the bedsheet,

I couldn't brush them off without first announcing, "What I am about to brush off my bed is eraser crumbs."

Understandably Rigney soon got a room of his own. So did I—on the north side overlooking, and overhearing, the busy Boulevard Jourdan. But I had a large balcony, in case I ever needed a large balcony to harangue a mob, or accept a few huzzahs as a bedbug exterminator.

And Virginia Woolf was right. Having a room of one's own is vital, even for a man. Mine gave me more tranquillity in which to recollect emotion, plus I no longer had to share the box of Purdy's chocolates that my mother sent me monthly to sustain my fat content. Room 19 was where I chronicled my first visit to Britain, a Christmas spent with my Aunt Pat, Uncle Alex and their twelve cats. My *Province* columns about that heady communion with the smell of boiled fish, and a bicycle tour of southern France, provided the slender substance of *The Roving I*, published by Ryerson Press in 1950, and winner of the Leacock Medal for Humour. I share the credit with *Cimex lectularius* ("a wingless, bloodsucking bug"—*Webster's Collegiate*).

Aside from *les punaises*, I had no Parisian adventures in bed during my year of residence. I apologize to you, the reader. I had not only opportunity, but ample example, to take advantage of the city's postwar libertinism, the racy reputation of the City of Light Fantastic, and unlace the stays of Canadian discretion. Let the libido loose, *chéri*, but I didn't.

Feeble excuse: the town was teeming with American writers—many of them financed, like me, by their veterans' grants and allowances—all eager to emulate Ernest Hemingway. You couldn't get into Left Bank bistros like Les Deux Magots, because every table was taken up by Yanks lipping a Gauloise, sipping a Pernod, looking for someone to punch out, or for a *poule* to pick up, all in the cause of writing the great American novel of the 1950s.

Here were the raunchy Henry Millers in hot pursuit of the obliging Anaïs Nins. They sponged enough francs off admiring friends to jack up the prices of the Café de Flore. Canadian dissolute wannabes simply couldn't afford those Boulevard Montparnasse shrines of the lickerish literate.

Not being a novelist, I couldn't justify the dissipation. My interest was humour—punch lines, not punch-ups. Hence I sought out a personal icon: Art Buchwald. The American humorist, just starting his writing career, was the food and entertainment columnist for the international edition of the *New York Herald Tribune*. I made the pilgrimage to the *Tribune* office off the Champs Elysées in order to touch my idol's typewriter. Buchwald received me with more grace than had anyone at the Sorbonne. The rotund person in a corner of a small, grubby editorial room chatted with me as amiably as if I were somebody. A friendly bullfrog in a city of snapping turtles.

Somewhere in the editorial room of my mind, the decision was made: my future, if any, lay not in teaching but in writing.

Chapter 13

Adieu, Sorbonne

O ne evening in late 1949 I received a phone call at La Maison Canadienne. Astounding enough, one might say, given that I had no phone. But the miracle went beyond the connection with Alexander Graham Bell.

This call changed my life.

It was the only thing that I owed to the French telephone system which, as the wheeze went, is still in the experimental stage. But it was a biggie.

Madame had sent Claude to fetch me to the telephone in her office. A long-distance call from London! Madame hovered as I picked up the receiver, always alert to monitor the private lives of her residents. The call was from Bernard Braden.

"Eric, how would you like to write a radio show for us?"

"A radio show?"

"Barbara [Kelly] and I are in London and have interested the BBC in doing a half-hour comedy show called *Leave Your Name and Number*. It's based on our effort, as a couple of expatriate Canadians, to break into show business here. But we need a writer. Can you come over and write a pilot script? It'll be worth about fifty quid."

"There is a tide in the affairs of men, / Which, taken at the flood, leads on to fortune..." The trouble is, when we are standing in the water up to our hips, it is hard to tell whether the tide is coming in or going out. Were my affairs in flood? Or was fortune (fifty quid) poised to pull the plug?

My reply to Bernie was doubtless influenced by my growing disillusionment with the alleged doctorate. I had learned that the University of Paris—crafty old biddy that she was—had instituted two grades of doctorate: the *doctorat ès lettres*, a prestigious degree reserved for French students; and the *doctorat de l'Université*, awarded almost without fail to North American students feeding hard currency into France's piggy bank. The only candidate for the latter degree known to have received other than a pass with honours was an American who had pinched most of his thesis, verbatim, from a work by one of the professors giving the oral exam. They hated to do it, but they gave him only a passing grade.

"How soon," I replied to Bernie Braden, "should I get to London?"

As snap decisions go, it may not have been in the same class as Caesar's crossing of the Rubicon, but the English Channel was no slouch, either, in terms of casting the die.

A few days later I was sitting in the Bradens' apartment in Hampstead, waving bye-bye as they both went off to Portland Place for their interview with the BBC producer,

Light Entertainment. I had my fingers crossed that the enter-
tainment was light enough in the plot outline I had hastily
typed up for the assessment. I envied the Bradens their con-
fidence. They had left three small children in Toronto, where
they had established themselves as top-flight performers in
CBC radio drama, in order to take a flyer on the bigger time.
All three of us were West Coasters, Bernie's father being a
United Church minister in West Vancouver, and Barbara and
I both hailing from across Burrard Inlet. They were out to
conquer this Old World, and not a bitten nail in the lot.

We got the job. Suddenly I had sole responsibility for
scripting a thirteen-week series of what we now know as sit-
uation comedy. The sitcom was alien to the BBC in 1950. To
me, too. I literally didn't know what I was doing, and was
having to do it too fast to identify it.

Leave Your Name and Number was an instant success.
The show got good reviews from the London papers, writ-
ten by radio critics celebrated for their ability to flense a
show and use the blubber as fertilizer. Much of the Bradens'
triumph lay in their having a Canadian accent, acceptable to
all castes of a British audience split among Scottish come-
dians, North Country George Formbys, Cockney clowns and
Noël Coward's nobby crowd. Also, Canada had earned bags
of goodwill with its war effort to help defend John Bull from
Herr Moustache. *I* hadn't, but I felt no need to include this
fact in the show's credits.

The pace of events was too hectic for me to go looking for
accommodation in London. I moved in with Howard
Rigney's girlfriend, Margaret Benn. In retrospect I see that
this was not a victory for good judgement. Margaret shared
her Knightsbridge flat—a swank address—with two other
young women, one a willowy American beauty, the other an
English "land girl" who looked ready to be cultivated. Since

- 1 -

1	BARBARA	Wait, Bernie. I've just put on my new spring outfit. Like it?
2	BERNARD	(FLATLY) Uh-huh.
3	BARBARA	It's the new apron style. All the smart dresses have aprons this year.
4	BERNARD	Uh-huh.
5	BARBARA	I think this apron is awfully sweet, don't you?
6	BERNARD	Uh-huh.
7	BARBARA	All right, dear, you can go and wash the dishes now.
8	RONALD	Ladies and gentlemen, it's "Bedtime With Braden".
	MUSIC	THEME
9	BERNARD	Hello, this is Bernard Braden with another of the shows recently described as being like the Third Program.with the cultural value removed. And we've only just started, cosmically speaking. Any day now you'll see the name of the show in big letters in the Radio Time's listings, just like "Programme Parade", "General Weather Forecast" and the other top shows. The trouble has been that they don't give you big letters unless you have the Augmented Dance Orchestra directed by Stanley Black. Now, however, plans are completed for augmenting Nat Temple's band.
		(CONT. OVER.....

Excerpt, script from the radio show "Bedtime with Braden," 1951. Three Canadians invaded the BBC, taking no prisoners. (UBC) these stunners were having a problem raising the wind of rental, they found it expedient to sublet me the maid's room, a windowless, airless, phoneless cell, perfect for a troglodyte praying for one-liners. As there was no room for a bed, the women let me sleep on the sofa in their drawing room. It was a weekend arrangement that lasted four months.

I promptly fell in love with Margaret. This was consistent with my amatory performance, well expressed by the old song's lyrics: "If I can't be near the girl I love, I'll love the girl I'm near." I was near Margaret—a slim honey blonde whose short checked skirt and dark stockings introduced me to the unique sensation of actually feeling the pupils of my eyes dilate. Although born in Canada, she had come to Britain as the ward of English relatives who were landed gentry. She was definitely upper crust, whereas I was your basic open-face pie. Margaret's Mayfair accent challenged me to rise above my station, born on the wrong side of the tracks, now living in a country that didn't even have the same gauge railway. The classic elements of tragedy.

Such, I guess, is the cussedness of the human heart. Recently, after reading Michael Holroyd's biography of George Bernard Shaw, I was struck by Shaw's persistence in going after women that he knew he could not have, either because they were married or, like Mrs. Patrick Campbell, safely living in the United States. It may be a subconscious defence mechanism, a kind of auto-immunization against being permanently disabled by matrimony. I could make love to my best friend's fiancée because I was loyal enough to him to let her marry him. (As she eventually did.)

One weekend, given a breather from the typewriter, I accompanied Margaret on a visit to the country-gentry home of her uncle and aunt. These were her nearest relatives in the United Kingdom, and I was dimly aware that one purpose of the visit was the opportunity it gave her tweedy kin to assess this raw Canuck who had established a strange relationship with both their niece and Auntie BBC. Their scrutiny was, of course, discreet. Although, when I passed "Uncs" in the hall on the way to the bathroom, he seemed relieved to see that I came equipped with a civilized toothbrush, rather than a twig or something. In the morning he showed me his oasthouse in the back forty.

"That is where we dry the hops," he explained, gesturing at the structure with his cane.

"Looks a bit like one of our tepees," I observed.

He seemed disturbed by that comment, as if I might be tempted to sneak into his oasthouse for a quick drag on the sweetgrass.

Margaret's aunt was a tad more direct in the way she sized me up. I never shook the feeling that she might ask someone to open my mouth so that she could better examine my teeth. In fact, she did conclude one piercing glance at my face by murmuring to Margaret, "Well, dear, *les yeux sont vifs.*" The eyes were lively. By inference, the nose was deadly. The ears might support a bowler, but the chin belonged on another face entirely.

I never saw my report card. The ratings became irrelevant when Rigney arrived unexpectedly from Paris to reclaim his betrothed from his ex-roommate. I did the proper thing and goofed my chance to be a cad and a bounder by rogering the bird, an event that might have been of more historical interest, though not much. Instead, totally miserable despite the success of the Bradens' radio show, I said goodbye to Margaret and caught the first plane back to Vancouver. Howard didn't wave. On that Trans-Canada Airlines Northstar flight I found that the way to avoid airsickness was to have a large ingot of grief resting in your gut. This made violent turbulence quite welcome, really, since crashing in a fireball would be an attractive side trip.

My parents were baffled by my woe-struck visage. When I am glum, even my feet look suicidal. My mother treated me as she might an unexploded bomb: possibly a dud, but dangerous if still live.

This period of mourning that passed for a holiday was curtailed by phone calls from Bernie Braden in London, anxious for confirmation that I did intend to return to help write a new radio show born of the hit *Leave Your Name and Number.* I had a short spell of mooning around muttering, "Eat your heart out, Pagliacci!" Laughing on the outside, crying on the inside—it can give you the hiccups. So I climbed back into a Northstar for the sixteen-hour flight to London, determined to profit from this gig by seeing more of Britain than the interior of a maid's room, and making sure I was paying rent to someone without a damage deposit on my heart.

The name of the new show was *Breakfast with Braden.* Bernie had sold the BBC on the idea of a half-hour variety program of sketches interspersed with band and vocal numbers by Pearl Carr and Benny Lee. This was the same format as the CBC's *Stag Party,* which Braden knew he could be comfortable with. The other two writers were Frank Muir and Denis Norden, two six-foot-plus Brits. Frank was a wry ex-RAF officer whose bristling moustache was the only air filter conditioning the dilapidated studio on Old Bond Street. Denis, dark and Jewish and very quiet, provided the foil for Muir's outrageous assaults on the pedestrian. They were the most brilliant comedy-smiths I ever worked with, both going on to distinguished careers in television and published works.

The producer of *Breakfast with Braden* was a bespectacled,

briar-sucking, middle-aged elf with the same hairstylist as Albert Einstein. Pat Dixon was one of those renegade English eccentrics who were the salvation of the Commonwealth. His puckish sense of humour discomfited the stately BBC, like a burr under her girdle. His willingness to consider any expression of dementia as Light Entertainment was undoubtedly a factor in our show's relegation to a ramshackle studio a provident distance from Portland Place. If *Breakfast with Braden* became *too* rambunctious, causing a question to be asked in Parliament, the corporation could disclaim responsibility, blaming the outbreak of lunacy on the plumbing, the canteen food or both.

Pat Dixon later produced the immortal *Goon Show*, which unleashed the very special mental aberrations of Peter Sellers and Spike Milligan which, in turn, pioneered the bedlam genre that ultimately gave the world *Monty Python's Flying Circus*. In short, *Breakfast with Braden* was in excellent manic hands in the studio control booth, against whose back wall I stood weakly, sweating bullets lest the band not laugh at lines in the sketch I had written, and watching for the mad-scientist gleam in Pat's eyes that meant I had done my bit to overthrow the reign of reason.

My major contribution was born of ignorance of BBC protocol. Our show's announcer, Ronald Fletcher, epitomized the Holy Corp's cadre of radio announcers, those plummy voices that had done so much during World War II to help keep Britain sane and confident. Fletcher had the kind of delivery that might have inspired Kipling to write:

> If you can meet with Triumph and Disaster
> And treat those two impostors just the same...
> You'll be a Man, my son.

What makes a man concerning me less than what makes a buck, I hit Pat Dixon with a terrorist notion: "Let's give Ronald some lines."

In terms of enormity of concept this was like adapting the Albert Memorial to include a coconut shy. For a moment the sheer audacity shook my producer. Then his satanic eyebrows had an erection, the tobacco in his infernal pipe glowed incandescent and...a star was born. The unflappable Fletcher proved to have a streak of ham in him as broad as our comedy. He went on to a career in radio and television that earned him, when he died in 1995, quarter-page obituary tributes in the national press. By God, I had my Pygmalion!

For its estimated three million listeners, *Breakfast with Braden* quickly became as much a part of the British breakfast as Devon bacon and runny eggs. Radio was still *the* medium of popular entertainment in 1950. Private stations being outlawed, the BBC had a monopoly on its captive audience, which could choose between only a couple of national services. Result: public acclaim, if gained, soon became massive and mind-boggling. *My* mind was boggled big-time, not only by the knowledge that I was writing to be heard by enough people to populate one of our Prairie provinces, but also by the obese fee that my agent—to whom I had been introduced by Norden and Muir—had wangled for me. With two "repeats" the loot doubled and tripled. If I had had time to think about it, success could have turned my head, removing my nose from the grindstone. But I didn't, not after our show's broadcast was moved into the Paris Cinema, a large theatre on Lower Regent Street that the BBC rented for comedy shows deserving of a studio audience.

Henceforth, my material would need to elicit laughs not merely from the band's trombone player—who knew which side his crumpet was buttered on—but a disinterested house of several hundred civilians, each wearing a button that said Show Me.

I had no time to meditate on the irony that seven years of slogging it at French studies had brought me to the Paris Cinema. *Vive la France!*

Chapter 14

I Always Shop at Harrods

What had I learned as a doctoral candidate at the Sorbonne?

1. You can't beat a French bike for speed. Aluminum frame. Goes like a bomb, but lacks the robust thews of the old Raleigh.

2. The perspective of the straight, broad, tree-boulevarded avenue should culminate in an Arc de Triomphe. A street that merely feeds into a freeway is like making love without the climax. Vaguely unsatisfying.

3. The North American city's pattern of grid streets makes for a populace with the soul of a set square.

Most of the streets of Paris are as sinuous as the Seine itself. A nightmare for taxi drivers, but a figure of sensuous curves for the stroller.

4. It is okay to park one's car on the sidewalk if there is enough sidewalk left to park on. Canadian drivers are, literally, curbed by the gutter. To the Parisian, the curb is just one more thing to be mounted.

They say that everyone has two hometowns—his own and Paris. I doubt that Paris gives a damn—it's that kind of city—but I'm happy to be one of her foster children. When it comes to the ties of blood and birthright, however, London is my town. If I had to choose a city to live in without the humbling presence of mountain, ocean and rain forest, it would be Tiffin-on-Thames. The queen runs a neat neighbourhood. Or did in 1950. It was still the place of which Dr. Johnson said, "Any man who is tired of London is tired of living."

At mid-century, with her cratered blocks and battered streets still glowing with the victory of the Battle of Britain, London was as exhilarating as catching a big red double-decker bus while it was still moving, swinging aboard on the stanchion and being welcomed by the female conductor: "Mind your step, luv." The camaraderie of the war still poured out of every tube station. Even the pigeons of Trafalgar Square had legitimized their strut. Paris did not burn, and was the colder for it.

I had to find lodging. Fast. No more shacking up with other guys' betrothed. A rental agency referred me to a stately home-gone-rooming-house on Kensington High Street. My second-floor suite was the most spacious in the place, with its own kitchen and bathroom, roughly the equivalent, in Vancouver, of having a swimming pool and stables. Paying the rent was no problem. I lived like a lord among the house's motley collection of postal clerks and secretaries, inhabiting the unglorified closets of the original Georgian mansion. I got a lot of respect from those passing me on the oak stairs and felt fully competitive with the commissioner at Canada House. Yet I was careful not to put on airs. I didn't wear britches and slap them with a riding crop, or anything. I did buy an Aquascutum raincoat at Harrods, but I wore it only when provoked by humidity.

Even so, my digs were not a patch on the residence rented by the Bradens, a veritable estate, an oar's toss from Hampton Court, with lawns and gardens running down to nudge the storied waters of the Thames. The Bradens had been told by the agent that the house once belonged to Charles Dickens. Unlikely, but an ego-stroking thought whenever I visited the now-famous couple, and their three children, and was taken for a cruise upstream in the Braden launch through the hoary locks and fawning willows. Bernie and Barbara had lost no time in living up to their star status in the entertainment firmament of Britain. They were show people, and show it they did—their expensive cars, their clothes, and themselves—at the chic London clubs in company with the established, living icons of theatre and radio.

I, in contrast, squirrelled away my pay, rode the bus or underground and, perforce, limited my social activity to trying to seduce the more attractive female lodgers in my rooming house. My main charm was that my suite had a stove with an oven. All the women were wedded to tiny hot plates. If one of them wanted to roast a joint, or bake a pie, I was their sole recourse. Lord, what power! I was not above leaving my door open so that Hennie—the charming Dutch woman sharing the pigeon loft with two postal workers—

could smell my macaroni and cheese, fusing her fate with my largesse.

The strategy facilitated my introduction to Sheila, a former Miss England, now employed as a Palladium showgirl, making Heaven just one flight up from my oven trap. Legs without limit, a divorcée, Sheila had a wealthy patron who called for her in his Rolls-Royce, a fat little man who she told me was harmless, wanting her only to accessorize his appearances at social affairs where he wanted to impress people with his well-maintained virility. I believed her. I desperately *wanted* to believe her. When I heard her spike heels slowly mounting the stairs at two in the morning past my door, my entire being vibrated like a struck gong. And I would offer up a prayer that the fat little man would ask Sheila to bring a cake to his next party.

With Sheila I achieved a degree of sexual maturity. I wouldn't say that I graduated summa cum laude, but she did have the experience needed for advanced studies. An English war bride, she had divorced her Canadian commercial pilot after she discovered he had a problem holding course on fidelity when away from home.

"He told me he got awful headaches if he didn't have sex," Sheila told me as pillow talk. "So I gave him a headache he'll never forget."

Good man. Now, at last, *I* had what I'd always wanted: sex with my very own showgirl. For several weeks my daily exercise consisted of nipping up and down the stairs between Sheila's room and my own. I doubt that my oven's ultimate conquest was a secret to any of the other residents, but I was old-fashioned enough to be protective of a lady's reputation, regardless of the fact that she made a living by parading around London's largest stage wearing London's least costume.

Then, one morning when I had loped up the stairs to give Sheila her wake-up call—the reason why she called part of my anatomy "Little Ben"—I found her already dressed and entertaining a visitor. Her daughter, Valerie, was about five years old and had been living elsewhere with her grandmother. This was one of her periodic reunions with Mummy. She greeted me with a seasoned stare that unsettled me. I got the impression that she was accustomed to meeting strange gentlemen who romped into Mummy's room in their bathrobes.

"Valerie is staying with me for a while," Sheila said. "I hope you'll be friends."

The next morning it was I who was awakened—by Valerie. Her substantial body landed on my chest, scaring the daylights out of me.

"Good morning," she snarled.

I had difficulty budging the little brute off my thorax. "Good morning," I rasped. "Where's your—?"

"Mummy's gone out. She told me to come here. Let's play horsy! Giddyap!"

Valerie bounced on my belly. "Posting," I believe, is the equestrian term. I was shocked by the weight of the child, who had showed no overt sign of having an ass of solid lead.

This routine was repeated for several mornings. I was starting to dread the dawn. I was seeing less and less of Sheila, more and more of the Fifth Horseman of the Apocalypse.

Finally the penny dropped. I was being used. Not just my oven, but *me*. From intramural lover I saw myself degraded to built-in baby-sitter. In less stressful circumstances—my typewriter ribbon was jumping fourteen hours a day—I might have accepted the quid pro quo that some people call "a relationship." But on my tight schedule there was no room for Valerie on my stomach. I had to inform Sheila that I was retiring as nanny, stomping out of her room, never to ascend again. My fault, of course. I had tried to attain the Muslim paradise without having the decency to die first. The little fat man in the Rolls-Royce had a better grip on reality. My oven was not enough to qualify me for Sheila. When I was laid abed by the flu, it was Hennie, the nice Dutch woman, who brought me a bowl of onion soup. I hate onion soup, but I still love Hennie.

My spavined sex life was reflected in the sketches I was writing for *Breakfast with Braden*. In his own memoirs, *The Kindness of Strangers*, Bernie Braden observes: "The problem with Eric was that he was prone to sexual innuendo, although it was some time before anyone in the BBC noticed it, other than Pat Dixon who encouraged it."

At one point Bernie was summoned to the Olympian office of Michael Standing, head of BBC Light Entertainment, and asked to explain a section of dialogue from the previous week's script. When Bernie pleaded ambiguity of interpretation, Standing drew himself up to his considerable height in his royal-blue suit and announced, "Mr. Braden, in my capacity as head of Light Entertainment in the BBC, I want you to understand that I will not wear blue material." Exit Bernie, strangled by laughter.

Thereafter, Pat Dixon did his best to tone my off-colour blue lines down to a passable shade of blah. In his memoirs, which include several of my sketches that I had long since forgotten, Bernie cites an Uncle Gabby monologue in which I had him reminiscing about his days in the Yukon: "Those was tough times up there in those days. No women available. No, sir. About the only form of animal life was sheep. The most popular song that year in the Yukon was 'It Had to Be Ewe.'" Pat changed the spelling in the script to "You." It got past the censors without forcing me to grow up and out of my puns.

This wink-wink, nudge-nudge wordplay has plagued my editors in every form of writing I have attempted. Only recently have I abandoned my lame excuse ("Shakespeare did it, too"). I am too old to mature now.

But the phenomenon makes me wonder: are the authors of Harlequin romances compensating for their own sex life, which rates with bowling night for the emperor's eunuchs? Conversely writers from whom is never heard a scatological word are in private life satyrs and nymphs. They have got it all out of their system. If my theory is valid, Sir James Barrie was a sex pistol, while D.H. Lawrence wasn't getting any.

However, sensing that I was getting pretty strung out, the Bradens did their best to integrate me with English society. They got me invited to literati parties in Chelsea, which in the 1950s was the Bloomsbury of the 1920s. I failed to mingle. Mingling has never been my forte. Something about me acts as a conversation repellent. Other people have magnetic personalities; mine just points north.

On a different level of immaturity, I was beginning to chafe at the galley-slave status of the comedy scriptwriter. The credits voiced by the announcer at the close of the show registered with no one, I guessed, except me. Even my parents were not within range of the BBC transmitter. Of fame and fortune, I was missing the first f-word. My writing radio comedy sketches had won me membership in the Great Unwashed. Except for a few people within the broadcasting industry who knew that the funny lines didn't trip automatically off the tongues of the star performers, the obscurity was total. Who remembers the names of Jack Benny's writers? Or Bob Hope's? Their mothers, if reminded. And having tasted the sweet nectar of my byline on a newspaper column, accompanied by the photo to erase any doubt that I existed though spectral, I was doubly conscious of my gaining an insight into the identity problems of the Little Man Who Wasn't There. I was the living symbol of Canada—who he?

I might have been able to live with being a sort of tattletale grey eminence had not the scales fallen from my eyes in respect to the loot that was supposed to be compensating me for my labouring in limbo.

I was told about British income tax.

The government of the day was Clement Atlee's socialist horde. (God, how I missed Churchill!) Labour had ridden out of the north to rape and pillage higher-income earners, regardless of race, religion or reclusiveness. Not only was the income tax nineteen shillings and sixpence on the pound in my exalted bracket, but I learned to my horror that in the United Kingdom the queen's tax inspectors had the authority to check on one's bank account if they got a whiff of gamy return. *My* invisibility might be total, but the thousands of pounds I had socked away in the London branch of my Canadian bank would become common knowledge when I was arraigned before the Beak in the Old Bailey, charged with cheating the chancellor of the Exchequer.

Alternatively—and this thought gave me night sweats worse than those caused by Sheila's heels—I could pay my income tax. This prospect was so ghastly even to contemplate that I turned in desperation to the Bradens for a referral to a tax accountant with an English bloodline back to Merlin the Magician. The Bradens, I knew, were enjoying huge deductions for their expenses as performers—clothes, entertaining, publicity photos, et cetera—none of which accrued to a flat rat.

Bernie gave me the name and Mayfair address of his tax accountant, whom I'll call Mr. Murdstone. I was early for my appointment, as usual, but was eventually ushered into a large, oak-panelled chamber occupied by a massive desk and the silver-haired gentleman sitting behind it.

"Come in, Mr. Nicols," Mr. Murdstone said. His desk was clean but for a few ceremonial masks—immediate family, I assumed. "Do sit down."

I sat and blurted out my predicament. I had saved all this money, earned by the sweat of my muse, and now the government threatened to take all but sixpence away from me so that Mr. Atlee could nationalize the steel industry.

Mr. Murdstone listened patiently to this litany of grief, his hands clasped across his black-worsted vest, lips pursed in mild wonder. At last he spoke. "Yours is an extraordinary case, Mr. Nicols. Virtually all my clients in the entertainment profession, having spent all they have earned, come to me to help them convince Her Majesty that it is impossible to extract blood from a stone. I have never before encountered the phenomenon of a person in your profession improvident enough to have the wherewithal to pay his income tax."

I squirmed in my chair. Abnormal, that's what he was implying I was. A pecuniary pervert. Not fit to be in show-biz. Should never have been allowed to leave the colony. I snivelled, "Is there nothing you can do?" I must have sounded like Oliver Twist pleading for more swill.

"Well," Mr. Murdstone said with the inflection of offering a last resort, "you could buy diamonds."

I gaped with incredulity. "Diamonds?"

"Yes. They are a type of rare gem. Buying diamonds would clean out your bank account. The tax inspectors are not permitted to scrutinize your personal safe."

It didn't seem the moment to tell him that the only personal safe I owned was a Ramses older than its expiry date.

"Of course," he added, "you won't he allowed to take your diamonds out of the country."

"Buy diamonds," I said, nodding. "Just the job. Thank you so much, sir. I'll try to keep in touch." I departed, holding back the whimper until I was clear of his office.

I sat for a while on a bench in Green Park, contemplating the other sheep ready to be shorn. What I couldn't see was myself growing old in the service of the BBC, taking a break every six months or so to pour my diamonds over my head, cackling crazily. Much as I admired England and had relished bike rides to Stratford to view Shakespeare on his own turf, trips through the comely Cotswold Hills for the Malvern Festival of Shaw, and expeditions around the Hardy country of rugged Devon and Cornwall, rambles that enchanted me with the sheer poetry of the terrain and its villages, the chances of my ever being more than a diamond-laden alien were patently long-shot.

No one likes to admit that she or he is homesick. It smacks of defeat. If homo erectus had kept running back to his native savanna every time he felt homesick, Africa would now be bulging with six billion humanoids, while the rest of the planet would be as desolate as Labrador on a Saturday night.

I tried to rationalize the itch to ditch success, telling myself: "What you miss, old cock, is the West Coast wilderness. This country is too...occupied. It's a beautiful space, but none of it can be yours alone. Every forest, each mountaintop, any stream, belongs to someone, or everyone, who may appear abruptly to claim your tranquillity, your assurance of being one-on-one, up close and personal, with Mother Nature. What you miss is the facility to get lost in the woods, totally astray, five minutes' walk from Vancouver city limits..."

Excuses, excuses. I still had to contrive a breakaway spat with the Bradens to effect my escape from the diamond mine. Television aborning at the BBC, Bernie and Barbara were offered their own show on the ruptured rectangle. I agreed to write the show, but when the contracts came up for signing I demanded the same fee that each of the stars was to receive—an outrage roughly comparable to the butler's insisting on dining with the lord and lady of the manor. There was a nasty scene with Barbara, and I packed the Aquascutum, the old portable Underwood in its battered case and waved bye-bye to Eros in Piccadilly and to the oven that had been my Cupid. Britannia ruled the airwaves, but not my home and native land—Canada.

Chapter 15

Readmitted to the Printed Ward

Returning to Canada in 1951, I had enough credentials on my résumé as a hawker of hee-hee to be offered the job of resident humorist by both the *Vancouver Province* and the *Vancouver Sun*. The *Sun* made the more vigorous pitch for my services, but I was leery of the paper's reputation for rambunctious journalism. The paper battened on the ebullient likes of Pierre Berton and Jack Webster, writers and editors with a predilection for the sensational. People *shouted* at one another, I'd heard, in the *Sun*'s editorial room. If I shout, my voice cracks, as any waiter will tell you. I didn't raise my voice to be a columnist.

I went with the *Province*—sedate and strictly West Side. Not for this—excuse the expression—broadsheet were such solar flares as the *Sun*'s gratuitous photos of the "Girl of the

Day." It took about forty years, but today the *Sun* is the city's more dignified journal, while the *Province* is a lean tabloid for the cool set. I disclaim responsibility. During those forty years, I wrote 5,846 columns for the *Province*, initially five a week, later three a week, after retirement one a week, and finally one a month. I should have known that the job wouldn't last.

En route home to Vancouver from London, I stopped in Toronto long enough to be feted as the Leacock Medal winner (for *The Roving I*). Because Ryerson Press was the United Church's publishing house, the party was modelled on a church service: the ladies wore hats, the gentlemen didn't and my book was solemnly toasted with sacramental orange juice. The general manager, a former minister, rose to give the benediction, assuring the assembled faithful that the Ryerson publication list was strong enough, with God's help, to sustain the presence of a book of a humorous nature. To set an example of tolerance, the general manager attempted to make a joke. It succumbed, but out of respect we all laughed. I was not asked to read the lesson. I got the impression that the house feared I might make humour the subject of levity.

Especially intimidating for me was Ryerson's publicity person, Elsinore Haultain, a stately flack whose head was crowned with coil upon coil of golden hair—a Rapunzel who had never been called upon to let her hair down. But she did a hell of a job selling my books.

The editor in chief of Ryerson at that time was the much-esteemed Dr. Lorne Pierce, a champion of Canadian literature and founder of the Canadian Hearing Society. He was quite deaf, though I didn't learn this until he turned on the battery of his hearing aid to listen to what I had finished saying. The veneration in which the elderly Dr. Pierce was held by his staff, plus his "presbycusis," guaranteed that a publication party had little likelihood of getting out of hand. I have attended funerals that were more boisterous. When Mrs. Haultain handed me a plate, I wasn't sure whether I should put an offering in it or seek food.

It was Dr. Pierce who drove me to Orillia for the Leacock Award ceremony. He owned a large black sedan with plenty of room for other members of the Ryerson party, but all except me, it seemed, had declined to be his passengers, preferring to travel by bus, oxcart or on foot rather than step into the good doctor's Black Maria. I quickly found out why. The moment I closed the door on my front death seat, Dr. Pierce turned off his hearing aid, aimed the car north and clamped the pedal to the metal. Rigid in reaction to the blaring horns of motorists having the temerity to try to share the highway with our juggernaut, I understood why Dr. Pierce had killed his audio: he didn't want any distraction from the beeline to Old Brewery Bay. Not a word was spoken during those terrifying eighty-odd miles other than an occasional sanctified epithet from my pilot when a truck tried to play chicken with this ordained minister who was surer of arriving in Heaven than I was.

To stave off motion sickness, I closed my eyes and therefore recall little of that part of Ontario. I opened them to receive the Leacock Medal and sit listening to Stephen's brother George as he addressed the dinner audience and was funny enough to make me sick though motionless. He concluded by saying that he would like to introduce someone who was even more humorous than Stephen: their mother. But she was dead. At that stage I couldn't help feeling grateful that Mum had gone to that great improv comedy stage in the sky.

I have no memory of how I got back to Toronto—maybe

I hitchhiked—but I know I did not leave the Leacock estate by way of his family home.

"His son may throw a beer bottle at you from a window," a local warned me. Altogether the experience at Old Brewery Bay was unsettling.

Before I left Toronto, *Maclean's* commissioned me to go to Hollywood to interview film stars Leslie Caron and Groucho Marx. Why the editors thought that writing personal essays qualified me to do any profile but my own, I know not. But I was not about to let a little ineptitude deny me the entrée to the glamorous world of moviedom. So I hung a hard left at Vancouver and landed in Los Angeles, stark naked without sunglasses. My letter of introduction won me admission to the studio where Leslie Caron was starring in *Gigi*. She received me in her dressing room.

The approved descriptive word for Caron was *gamine*, i.e., more pert than pretty, but with a dancer's figure that eliminated any doubt about her gender. With me she seemed distracted as she went through the motions of the PR interview. I tried to establish a rapport by addressing her in French—the first practical application of my years of extending fluency beyond *La plume de ma tante est sur la table*. I told her I had seen her in Paris when she was one of *les rats du ballet* at the Théâtre Roland Petit before she was "discovered" by Gene Kelly, who gave her instant international fame as his dancing partner in *An American in Paris*.

Leslie did not appear pleased by this reminder of her past. Later I was to learn that she was currently engaged to the scion of an American meat-packing corporation—M. Hormel. Instead of reminding her of Gene Kelly I should have been asking her about her feeling toward tinned ham. Sensing I had put my foot in something dismal, I cut the interview short before I drew tears and was thrown off the

Interviewing lovely Leslie Caron in her Hollywood dressing room, 1951. My French got me nowhere. (BCBW)

lot for harassing a star.

As for Groucho, I was surprised to find that his home stood on a lot not much larger than a standard Vancouver fifty-footer. I had been expecting an estate with a fair hike up the driveway and flunkies touching their caps when I produced an exclusive entrée to Marx Mansion. But, no, Groucho, a bespectacled, elderly man without the paint-on-moustache or any other indication of Marxist madness, answered the doorbell himself.

"Hmm, *Maclean's*," he said, reading my letter of introduction. He pronounced the name of Canada's best-known magazine as "Macleens," like the toothpaste. He didn't bother to try to pronounce mine. "Come on in."

I don't know why I half expected to see Groucho lope about the house in that low crouch, mouthing his phallic cigar and searching for prey that resembled Margaret Dumont, that large and regrettably dignified lady who for years suffered atrocities wreaked upon her by the berserk brothers. Certainly I was not prepared for the solemn gentleman who invited me to join him upstairs, he riding the funicular that made the ascent something of an ascension, a rising above any hope I had of noting down zingy one-liners for my article.

Groucho led me into a child's bedroom. (This was not going well at all.) Never one to adjust readily to the unforeseen, I made the mistake of asking, "What are your current interests, Mr. Marx?"

Pencil poised over notebook, I was appalled to hear Groucho launch into an extended monologue about his four-year-old granddaughter, Melanie. Or it may have been Maladie. Whatever, much as I might admire his devotion to this intrusive brat, the scene was in dire need of Harpo's marching in, his klaxon quacking to galvanize the Dean of Put-downs. Before I could turn the talk to a generation that was toilet-trained, an aide summoned Groucho to the film crew set up in his drawing room, which explained why I had been diverted to the loft. As I was being shown out by the aide, I could hear Groucho snapping off thigh-slappers for the camera to audience laughter cut off by the door closing behind me.

Needless to say, neither of my articles was used by *Maclean's*. This truncated my career as a Hollywood reporter. I had learned that it takes a special skill to ask the right questions, be unobtrusive about registering the answers and prepare to set up light housekeeping in the interview room until the subject at last tires and says something he or she didn't mean to. Hopefully within the week.

I returned to Vancouver, and to writing about the person

I knew best—not well, but better than Hollywood celebrities: myself.

The front-page column the *Province* gave me was headed "Eric Nicol," an index of how highly regarded newspaper columnists were by the trade at mid-century. The papers were so competitive—being mostly independently owned—that the publishers had to put up with egocentric, opinionated codswallop on pages held too respectable today outside the sports section. So I lucked out. The two Vancouver dailies were locked in a titanic struggle for the best funnies, and my copy helped to give the edge to the Katzenjammer Kids.

Today most senior newspaper executives, having come up through the ranks of the company's advertising or managerial branches, tend to view the columnist as a necessary evil. If they had their druthers, they would limit opinion to the editorial page where it can

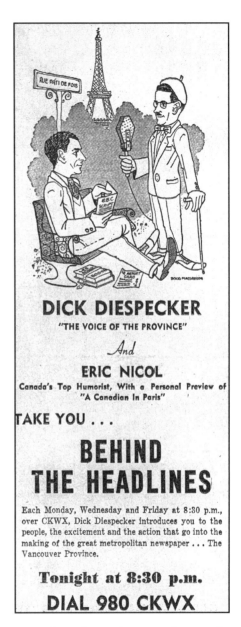

DICK DIESPECKER
"THE VOICE OF THE PROVINCE"

And
ERIC NICOL
Canada's Top Humorist, With a Personal Preview of
"A Canadian In Paris"

TAKE YOU . . .

BEHIND
THE HEADLINES

Each Monday, Wednesday and Friday at 8:30 p.m., over CKWX, Dick Diespecker introduces you to the people, the excitement and the action that go into the making of the great metropolitan newspaper . . . The Vancouver Province.

Tonight at 8:30 p.m.
DIAL 980 CKWX

My radio talks in the 1950s hastened the popularity of television. TV gave me gas. (UBC)

be reached only after a proper meeting. Otherwise it is an uncontrolled substance. If a personal column cannot be eliminated because it is popular with readers, at least it can be placed in the paper where it is least likely to create addiction.

I have done some shameful things in my life, but I have never been part of a consensus.

One day, after I had been writing the daily column for about twenty years, the publisher of the *Province* called me into his inner sanctum, sat me down and said, "Eric, surely you don't want to be a columnist all your life."

"I don't?"

"No. We're offering you the position of editor of the editorial page."

The ball had come out of left field, but I had no problem with the catch. "Thank you, sir, but in my opinion there are only two worthwhile jobs on a newspaper—columnist or the publisher. And I don't think you're ready to retire."

The publisher nodded, and since I expected no apology, I left. Immediately thereafter my daily column was cut back to three a week, a pruning that shocked my top growth but didn't affect the root system. Actually I was glad to share my space with humorist Hymie Koshevoy, a builder of puns of mass destruction, beside which mine looked like Oscar Wilde gone mild.

Among the many professional clubs of which I have never been a habitué is the Vancouver Press Club. For years the Press Club was avoided by *all* bona fide journalists, because admittance was not restricted to members only, and there was every chance that a crusading newsman might receive a knuckle sandwich, delivered by an aggrieved reader.

Anyway, humorists are not clubbable. The only other member of the journalist breed whom I met with socially was the *Province*'s Jim Taylor, the best Canadian sports-writer ever to merrily purée an overmuscled professional ego.

Jim and I met regularly. Not over a shot glass but a bag of oranges at the Southlands Elementary School playing field, where our same-age sons—Chris and Chris—played community-league soccer every Saturday morning (in season). My Chris's team was sponsored by the Nightingale Pharmacy, so I could be heard yelling, "Come on, Nightingales!" But not often.

Dads who stand in the mud together, experiencing the agony of defeat without the sorehead bellow that defines the parental goon—that's bonding. I have a lot of time for Jim Taylor, as does his enormous readership.

Another eminent Pacific Press colleague, whose name I glumly crossed off my Christmas card list, was Clyde Gilmour. In the 1950s Clyde was writing theatre reviews in the same season that I was researching a potential wife that my mother had recommended. Barbara Donald was the manager of The Bay's book department, and Mom saw her as a sensible, though attractive, helpmate for her inextricable boarder.

On one of my dates with Barbara, at a party, I introduced her to Clyde. I learned later that she quickly won his heart by giving him the perfect gift: a pen flashlight that would enable him to make notes in a darkened theatre.

Damn, I was too slow. Barbara married Clyde, and for years in Toronto was his girl Friday during his decades of good-humored hosting of the nationally popular CBC Radio program, *Gilmour's Albums*.

As Cupid, I was definitely good at shooting myself in the foot.

I now had time to diversify—even as recommended by

Judging beauty contests—another cross to be borne like a little soldier. This one took place in about 1963.

our business-page investment adviser. The writer who puts all her/his eggs in one basket may find that he/she is an ostrich. A bit cramped. Better, for me at least, was to have several baskets and one egg, hard-boiled enough to get slam-dunked game after game.

For one layup I was teamed with Norman Campbell. Norman was starting his career with the CBC, and together we contrived a couple of the corporation's earliest ventures into hour-long television productions: *The Big Dig* and *Make for the Woods,* the latter introducing a young singer named Robert Goulet.

No assignment was too bizarre for me to turn it down unless I was to be paid with beads and trinkets. A shamelessly commercial hack, I did everything from composing the epigraph for a local restaurant's placemats—a merry diner is less likely to notice that the grub in his green salad is alive—to the continuity for the Vancouver Diamond Jubilee extravaganza staged in Stanley Park's Brockton Point cricket field.

I sat in on the meeting where the show's "director general," specially imported from Texas to create epic proportion, tried to persuade us natives that the climax of the show—which had a cast of 5,000 and an outdoor "stage" 515 feet long—should be a reproduction of Vancouver's Great Fire of 1886. This, he assured us, could be achieved by setting ablaze the forest atop the North Shore mountains. There's no question it would have been a spectacular backdrop, one to make Cecil B. DeMille himself bite his riding crop. Unfortunately the municipalities of West and North Vancouver objected to being torched. Another disappointment was that the show's opening night was rained out, shortly after American comedy star Eddie Cantor roared in from the wings in a jeep and got mired in the mud of the rugby field.

Being a dilettante writer was easier in those days because I could breathe without having to join a union. Being a member of the Newspaper Guild was an option only, for columnists, perhaps because the union could never make up its mind on whether we were blue-collar or turtleneck. During my forty years of column writing for the *Province,* I never had a contract, being too shy to ask for one myself, and too cheap to hire an agent. I was neither labour nor management. Whenever the paper was hit by a strike, I just picketed my den at home and yelled, "Scab!" when the cat barged in.

Result: I never took a holiday and never missed a deadline, having stacked a reserve of enough columns to feed the paper unless I came down with a terminal case of writer's block. I stayed in the public eye like Mighty Mote. Deplorable, but a living.

I was back living with my parents again in Point Grey. Nicol, the bad penny. As a boomerang kid, I was starting to lose some of my novelty value, especially for my father. Neither World War II nor BBC canteen food had insured that I would not be back in his house. Not because of unemployment, but from sheer convenience. True, living in my folks' home restricted my sex life to my car, either front seat or—a more serious affair—the back seat. On the other hand, I saved a lot of time on laundry.

But I was now thirty-two years old, the age when a man's mind is turned, with an ugly ratcheting, to thoughts of "settling down." Two things settle down: men and dregs. I fitted the description of both. It never occurred to me that I might be able to live with a woman without first marrying her, with all that this meant in becoming a breadwinner: having to win more bread, and maybe give up doughnuts. Hey, the idea scared me. Telling a girl "You are the loaf of my life"— no, I didn't want to say it, or hear it. An even bigger no-no was my living common-law. The operative phrase in 1952 was "living in sin." No way could I look deep into a woman's eyes and say, "I'd like to live in sin with you. Your place or mine?" It wasn't in the cards, but the dealer, Time, was waiting for me to bet.

The *Province* having provided me with an office, I was there often enough to consider some of the female staff as my possible wife and mother of no children. However, it is not easy for the professional humorist to date. He, or she, has no way of telling whether someone of the opposite gender—or, I suppose, the same gender—is smiling at him or her as a sexual overture, or just because they have read something they found funny.

This is a cross I have borne all my adult life: the cursed ambivalence of a woman's smile. The better known you are as a humorist, the farther you have to travel—in severe cases into the Amazon jungle—to be certain the smile you get is not related to your work. Even then it may mean only that your fly is open.

This, I submit, is one reason why the humorist's private life is apt to be a train wreck: the signals get crossed. Small wonder, then, that so many humorists have been heavy drinkers. Stephen Leacock, Don Marquis, Robert Benchley, James Thurber, W.C. Fields—they all found trust in booze because the grape smiles impartially at us, regardless of our colour, sex, or books in the humour section of the public library.

One also understands why the humorist uses a nom de plume—"Molière" or "Saki," for instance. A wise clown never gives his right name.

At any rate, I was still a single white male in 1953 when the *Province* sent me to report on the social event of the year: Queen Elizabeth II's visit to Fiji. The occasion took on special importance since stress cracks were appearing in the British Empire. India had gone with Nehru, and African colonies were rocking the Raj. Now the young Elizabeth, newly married to the dashing Prince Philip, was sailing in her seagoing palace, the royal yacht *Gothic*, to this cluster of South Pacific isles whose fealty was total. The world's press was agog, and I bought a new pair of khaki shorts to blend with the coconuts.

Thanks to Dramamine, flying was no longer for me a case of breakfast revisited. The pills did have a soporific side effect, however, which made the stopover in Hawaii an interval of orchid-scented sleepwalking. But I was wide awake on the second leg to Fiji when our Canadian Pacific Airlines four-prop Britannia behaved naughtily, given the number of media passengers aboard. One of the stewardesses (now flight attendants with lower heels) had taken the seat beside me—yes, smiling—and we were chatting when I noticed flame shooting out of a port-side engine. I let her finish her remarks about my column, then pointed out the window, saying, "Should there be flames shooting out of that engine?"

"God!" The stewardess jumped up and ran to the cockpit, a clear indication that my question had not been rhetorical. For some reason I was not terrified by the sight of my plane's engine previewing Hell. Having been denied the opportunity to crash in flames as a pilot during the war, I saw it fitting that I should fulfill that destiny now over the South Pacific. As a service to the monarch en route to Fiji, it was a bit skimpy. But it was better than dying in a car crash near Spuzzum, British Columbia.

In a matter of seconds, the engine's flames turned to smoke and the prop stopped turning. My stewardess returned to the cabin, shaken but resolute, to announce, "Ladies and gentlemen, we have had a little engine trouble. We will be making an emergency landing at Christmas Island. Please fasten your seat belts."

She didn't tell us that Christmas Island was actually an atoll, a minuscule mound of coral close enough to the Equator to broil an iguana. Since this was the first time ever that the huge Britannia had tried to make a forced landing on Christmas, no one would bet that the plane wasn't longer than the atoll—a lively challenge to the plane's braking system.

Here it was December, and Christmas was coming at about 100 feet per second.

Stopping just short of a welcoming party of one palm tree, the aircraft disgorged its passengers onto the deserted runway. Then we heard the pilot tell us, "The fire is out, but we have to wait here till they can install a replacement for the fire extinguisher." (This was before airplane engines had sprinkler systems.)

"How long will that take?" someone asked.

"Hard to say. They have to fly one in from New Zealand."

Normally, when my vehicle is found to need a part that has to be flown in from New Zealand, I call a cab and go home. On Christmas I could call a crab, but the meter would kill me.

While we waited on the baking tarmac, I had ample time to reflect on how fortunate Robinson Crusoe was to be marooned on a desert island that wasn't more desert than island. It was ten hours before a flying boat delivered the fire extinguisher. Our pilot refused my request that they use it to put out my nose. Eventually we were once more on our way to Nadi, but my stewardess avoided me on this last leg. She probably knew a fire hazard when she smelled one.

At Nadi I was met by a phalanx of Fijian policemen in snaggle-toothed skirts. The other passengers seemed to think the honour guard of Melanesian fuzz was for them, too. Here I should observe that none of us laughed at these cops in frilly kilts, because Fijians are *big*. They are a happy, friendly people who can be that way because they are *very, very big*. This is why Fiji's rugby team qualifies to compete in world cup events. If Canada could find out what makes

Fijians so enormous, sans steroids—burly genes, a taro-root-and-whale-meat diet, whatever—our football, basketball and hockey teams could dispense with importing American brawn.

Okay, so maybe their having been cannibals not too long ago has something to do with their being *big*. Let's not get preachy about a diet supplement that might transmute Canada's bronze medal to gold. It was for the *mana*, or warrior spirit, that Fijians used to pop their defeated foe into the pot. Adopting this procedure may require a slight addition to National Hockey League penalty rules, but the governors would likely buy it.

Anyway, those big Fijian policemen ensured that our international press corps, when assembled in the capital city of Suva, was the best-behaved bunch of newshounds ever to stay on command. We were billeted in a private girls' school vacant for the Christmas holidays. My cot was handy to a sign on the wall: If You Need a Mistress, Ring the Bell.

Needless to say, I didn't get much sleep, what with smart alecks hopefully pushing the button. This activity was accentuated by the media welcoming party, which introduced us to kava. A Fijian drink made from the root of the *yanggona*, kava has much the same effect as being shot with a tranquillizer dart. The mind remains clear, but the legs suddenly give way, leaving the drinker prostrate but fully capable of regretting his choice of beverage.

Kava has the same appearance and taste as carbolic soap—shaken, not stirred. For ceremony, it is served in a *big* wooden bowl, which must be drained in one gulp lest the host be offended, with consequences mentioned above concerning Fijian eating customs. When my turn came, I had a bit of trouble (gagging) sipping the sudsy detergent, snorting the dregs into my sinuses which, I had to admit, remained clear for months afterward.

As for our young queen, when it came *her* time to chugalug the kava at the huge rally in Albert Park, she, too, had to pause in mid-gulp, causing a near-coronary in us whites amid a mass of half-naked Fijian warriors in full martial mode—spears, clubs, the lot. They included "bush boys" from the outer islands who had arrived in Suva harbour aboard crude catamarans, whose sails appeared to me to be made of skin—whose, I didn't want to know. Luckily Prince Philip made up for Her Majesty's gaffe, almost swallowing his bowl entire and drawing an approving grunt from thousands of throats, a sound that shook coconuts off palms a mile away.

Such were the sacrifices made by that royal couple whose children have proved, a half century later, to be unworthy. None of us who observed the unfailing graciousness of the queen in the hammering heat as she was driven over miles of dusty roads, while we ink-stained rabble squirmed in our neckties, could be other than totally smitten by respect. Had I known what was going to happen I might have slipped Phil a condom.

As if touring Viti Levu were not test enough, the queen and her escort elected to make the considerable side trip to Tonga. Tonga's Queen Salote had been the hit of Elizabeth's coronation parade in London—a *big* woman riding in an open carriage despite the pelting rain. Elizabeth owed her one. Some of us press folk preceded her to Tonga in a Royal New Zealand Air Force flying boat, I being lured by the promise of meeting the royal turtle. This turtle was reputed to be centuries old, alive when Captain Cook visited Tonga in 1773. I saw the opportunity for a unique interview.

"Tell us, Mr. T., what was your impression of—"

"*Mrs*. T."

"Oh, I beg your pardon. What was your impression, ma'am, of Captain Cook?"

"He seemed a nice enough fellow. Of course, I only saw him up to his knees."

"Oh, right."

"And I was laying an egg on the beach at the time."

"Sort of put you off tourists, did it?"

"Hate the buggers. Excuse me."

So I never got to meet the Cook turtle. In fact, the queen's party stayed in Nuku'alofa only long enough to meet the monarch, have lunch and watch a bevy of charming Tongan girls do a dance that involved only the upper part of the body—eminently sensible, in my view. After the royals departed, our press gang was ferried out to the waiting Sunderland, which bore us aloft, stalled as though really reluctant to leave such an amiable atoll, then slowly spiralled back down onto the lagoon.

"Sorry, chaps," the pilot said. "Spot of engine trouble. Afraid you'll be spending the night here."

Twice in one trip! Someone Up There seemed to want to keep me Down Here.

For most of the reporters the enforced respite was a welcome opportunity to discover, off the record, just how friendly the Friendly Islands could be. The London *Times* man was particularly enterprising in finding a night's lodging in one of the town's more accommodating native huts. The American journalists, too, disappeared into sites not on the official itinerary. Ever slow off the mark, I allowed myself to be directed to the home of the British commissioner. I could tell, from his manner of receiving an uninvited Canadian newsperson, that he would need to have the place fumigated after I left. I spent an unfulfilling night on the sofa.

When, in the morning, our aircraft finally made it up and away, I thoroughly resented the satisfied smiles on the faces of my companions as they slept the 400 miles back to Suva.

Chapter 16

Move Over, Miguel de Cervantes

Befo re returning to Vancouver I took a couple of days' R and R at Korolevu, the paradisal resort up the coast from the capital. En route, my cab passed a roadside object, a six-foot-high obelisk, worn and weathered, that I took to be an ancient mileage marker.

"No, sir," my East Indian driver said. "That is a phallic stone. In the old days the Fijian warriors smashed their captives' brains out against those stones. It gave them strength."

It gave me pause. Here I had been knocking my own brains out, telegraphing dispatches to the *Province*, with no phallic benefit whatever. Sitting alone on Korolevu's rosy

When Captain Fracas died, I lost my best friend. I find it harder to relate to people.

coral beach, watching the unspeakable sunset gild the lagoon, listening to the hermit crab (my role model?) scuttle from shell to shell, I knew that something had to be done about my still being a spinster. Not a bachelor. Bachelors have more fun, lying abed in a *mbure* scented with hibiscus blossoms, palpating a pawpaw redolent of a firm, young breast.

I talked to the gecko—green, bug-eyed, glue-footed— above my head. "I'm about ready to join you on the ceiling, Liz. Save me a gnat."

Those were my sentiments on my return to wintry Vancouver. And yet the caveat haunted me. Said Francis Bacon: "He that hath wife and children hath given hostages to fortune."

When the man is a newspaper columnist, living by his wits or whatever facsimile his mind can muster, his becoming a husband and father furnishes fortune with hostages guaranteed to last for the life of the idiot. And, face it, I was now committed to walking the tightrope daily, with the bridge of academe burning behind me.

The insecure nature of my vocation was underlined by an episode in 1954. For some reason unknown to medical science I started writing the odd column to be taken seriously. For a humorist this is substance abuse. His readers, if any, rarely appreciate it. When the Fool tries to play Lear, the whole play falls apart.

The moral issue that got me into trouble was capital punishment. Canada was still hanging convicted murderers in the 1950s, and I got it into my head that this was a travesty of justice. Not being a Christian, I believed that an eye for an eye, a tooth for a tooth, was a treatment better left to the ophthalmologist and the orthodontist.

The case that activated the impulse to self-destruct was that of a young man named Gash (unfortunate choice of cognomen) who had been found guilty of murdering a man on a local golf course. The sentence—hanging—made sense to a lot of golfers, the choice of the crime site being a kind of sacrilege. But to me, a duffer as well as a devout determinist, the hemp smacked of the medieval. Hard upon the verdict being announced, I wrote a column that was a parable based on the injunction "Thou shalt not kill." I had the Gash trial judge and jury arraigned before the court of Heaven, charged with murder. Superheated stuff, it was, proving that when you have a fire in the belly, smoke gets in your eyes.

Aware that my editor, Torchy Anderson, might detect an element of disrespect for the law in my diatribe, I sneaked the column into editorial on the weekend so that it went straight to the printers and hit the streets on Monday, steaming sacramental piss and vinegar.

"I opened a file," the paper's lawyer told me later, "as soon as I'd read your column."

Contempt of court. That was the charge that came thundering down from the bench. Although the case was to all intents and purposes closed, the judge had not yet dismissed the jury. A technicality, yes, but one upon which I could be hung, as on a butcher's hook, and for as long as m'lord took umbrage at my suggesting that he, and his jury, had violated one of God's commandments and might be barred from the celestial members' lounge.

The *Province*'s publisher and editor—also named in the indictment for contempt, although neither had had a chance to intercept the bombshell—sided with the lawyers in recommending that the paper publish an apology. Prominently. Maybe I could deliver it to the judge personally in my mouth. My response to this strategy of grovelling was to quit. Incredible as it seems now, this created a problem for Management. Indecision reigned. Public interest ballooned. Wire services hummed from all parts of the dominion for the latest word.

Kindly friends pointed out to me that I could be jailed and kept in the slammer until I purged the contempt, which could take more than boosting the prune juice. This motivated me to consult an old UBC friend, Les Bewley, who practised law.

"I don't trust the paper's lawyers to point out to the judge that he's an asshole," I told Les. "What do you think about my insisting on representing myself at the trial?"

Les, a laconic student of the human comedy, said, "The person who acts as his own lawyer has a fool for a client."

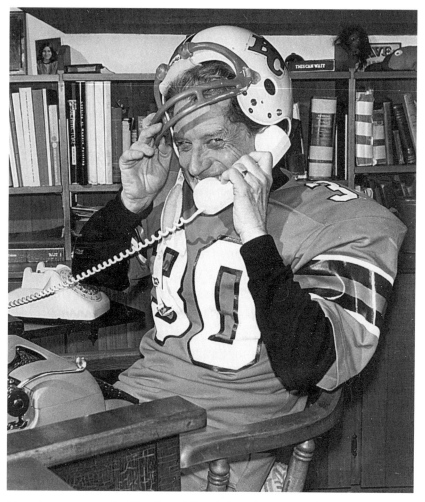

Mugging a promo for The Joy of Football, *1980. Jersey borrowed from BC Lions' Jim Young (Dirty Thirty). (UBC)*

Thus discouraged, and to my everlasting regret, I sat like a decoy duck, mute in a courtroom crowded with lawyers, law students and journalists, all attracted by what had become a cause célèbre across Canada. I cringed to hear what I had feared: our company solicitors sucking up to the bench so hard the judge had to hang on to his gavel.

The judge was J.V. Clyne, whose middle name was Valentine, although few people who had crossed him associated him with the saint of love. Clyne did look a bit like an overblown Cupid, but his bow and arrows were reserved for the death penalty. Before the trial one of the paper's lawyers confided to me that Clyne had been urged to throw the book at us, by A.M. Manson, also known as the "Hanging Judge," a title inherited from Matthew Begbie. The inference: don't be surprised, Nicol, if you find yourself standing on the trapdoor beside murderer Gash. You may be given the privilege of swinging first.

As it turned out, Clyne fined the paper and me a few thousand dollars. The *Province*, having had good value for its money in terms of public attention, insisted on paying my fine. Again my resistance was feeble. I was shedding integrity like a chicken in moult.

Taking their cue from Judge Clyne, all the jurors in the Gash case sued the paper and me for libel. Here was my chance to go to jail as a bankrupt. However, this civil suit was heard by Justice W.O. Wilson, who apparently had less affection for Canada's official hangman. When I rose—at last!—in my own defence, he waved me down, smiling, and dismissed the case. Rats. His decision was later reversed by the BC Court of Appeals, whose heart belonged to the hemp. This cost Southam Inc. several thousand dollars more, and me countless nights of lying awake composing immortal, Dreyfus-like statements to the Supreme Court of Canada. But the case never got that far. More rats.

Oh, how we stew in juices of our own making!

In retrospect I still regret my failure to become a martyr in a good cause. I let cooler heads prevail—a surefire way of earning obscurity. Instead of burning as a Joan of Arc, I had

For the sake of argument

ERIC NICOL SUGGESTS

If hangings continue— make them public

TORONTO (CP) — A record crowd of 28,000 last night watched Joseph Doaks die on the gallows in Varsity Stadium. The first person to be publicly hanged under floodlights — to accommodate those fans who work during the day — Doaks met death calmly.

The event was televised by the CBC for out-of-town viewers, and in the ratings topped Ed Sullivan's show . . .

Facetious? Not at all.

I suggest that the public hanging is the logical desideratum for those who would retain capital punishment as a deterrent—still a majority of Canadian citizens, according to the most recent public-opinion polls.

It is true that lately the Governor-General-in-Council has commuted to life imprisonment about ninety percent of death sentences. But Mr. Justice A. M. Manson of B. C. has damned this practice as flouting the law of the land, which is firmly backed by the belief, virile both in parliament and among the public at large, that the death penalty must be kept on the books for its effect as a deterrent.

No other defense

No other argument for c.p. remains respectable. The eye-for-an-eye chestnut has been generally repudiated as an attempt to find divine sanction for an act of pure revenge.

As chastisement the death penalty is even less defensible, being a corrective whose benefits to the offender are singularly short-lived.

In short, unless it is a deterrent the gallows — or the electric chair, or the gas chamber — is nothing. Nothing, that is, but a brutal vengeance, a killing whose agony of suspense far exceeds any-thing the condemned person may have perpetrated.

Then should not the deterrent be as widely publicized as possible? If the state is to take a human life, should not this precious appropriation be exploited to the full measure of its value as a warning?

Our medieval ancestors were more sensible about this, not only hanging their victims in public but also drawing and quartering them. Cutting down the hanged man while there was still the breath of life in him, disemboweling and dismembering him — who could ask for a more specific deterrent than this.

Yet, on evidence, these grisly exhibitions did nothing to discourage crimes of murder and theft among the rowdies, or treason in the mighty. As Arthur Koestler reminds us in his Reflections on Hanging, at that time when thieves were hanged for their crime, the crowd milling about the scaffold was thoroughly worked over by packs of pickpockets.

However, this is a departure from the point of my thesis. Merely as an aside I mention that some of us believe that capital punishment fails to justify itself as a deterrent, that most capital crimes are acts of blind passion or stupidity or bank robber's panic that never reckon the consequences. Just let it be footnoted that these crimes are controlled by social, psychotic and economic factors rather than the threat of the gibbet, as is easily demonstrable from the moderate crime records of countries (total: thirty-three) that have abandoned legalized killing.

End of digression. We'll assume now, for the sake of argument, that hanging is a deterrent, and I shall try to persuade you, if you are not already convinced, that the vulturous scaffold and its performance should be seen by as many potential murderers as possible.

I anticipate the objection that a public hanging would draw no audience, in this day and land of greater sensibility, and that the public en masse would turn a shuddering back on the terrible sight.

However, I believe I am correct in saying that the largest single crowd—well over 100,000 annually—to attend a sports event on this conti- continued on page 41

Inside every humorist lurks a preacher, chafing to attack Evil head-on. Maclean's published this piece on capital punishment in 1959. (UBC) incurred a hotfoot. Who remembers?

The compensation: Clyne's judgement in the case is still studied by law students as a classic of irrelevance. And the law has been changed to allow an appeal on conviction for contempt of court. And Parliament put paid to capital punishment in Canada. I take full credit for all three advances of civilization.

During the 1950s, I suffered another lapse into social crusade. New figures calculated by the World Health Organization indicated that the planet's human population was increasing at an exponential rate, and by the year 2100 we could be standing on one another's shoulders just to get a good view of doom. And I was already having trouble finding parking space.

After my quick change in a phone booth, I sprang forth with a column suggesting that Canada, being relatively inactive reproductively, should lead the way in educating the world's teeming hordes to find some alternative kind of recreation. If ice hockey was impractical in places like Africa, there was always Scrabble.

The column was timely enough to get the attention of a United Church minister named Oliver who wrote to me urging that we form a genuine organization that would actively promote birth control pole to pole. Even though it meant possibly losing the pope as a reader, I was messianic enough to use my column to recruit other apostles for what I dubbed the Society for Population Control (SFPC).

Very quickly I sucked into this black hole of a mission distinguished persons from several disciplines: Dr. Hugh Keenleyside, former director general of the United Nations Technical Assistance Administration; Dr. James Miller, head of genetics research at the University of British Columbia; P.R.U. Stratton, a prominent animal-rights activist; and a half-dozen other humanists who misjudged the power of the press when exerted by a known wag.

The SFPC held enough meetings to find a powerful sponsor in the Cadbury Society of Great Britain, whose philanthropic family was underwriting planned-parenthood programs abroad in order to create an empire where union jacking was modified by use of the diaphragm.

I soon learned that it was a mistake to take money from people whose wealth was based on the craving for sweets. To this day I wince at movie ads for *Like Water for Chocolate*. I'm reminded that my Society for Population Control got commandeered by the Cadburys, becoming the Planned Parenthood Association of British Columbia which, of course, still thrives today, tossing condoms like caramel gobstoppers to a population that nonetheless swells as the fat lady sings.

That ended my crusade to abate the Earth's surfeit of homo sap. The pen may be mightier than the sword, but it can't lick the penis.

The SFPC episode was to hang like a defunct albatross around my waist, the exercise having been endorsed by my own resolve to remain childless. Why? Because I am allergic to baby talcum? Not entirely. The main reason: I was a Canadian writer. Worse, I had been identified as a professional humorist, one trade that makes tightrope walking between tall buildings look like a sinecure.

No way did I have the credentials to be a family breadwinner. The crusts, maybe. As a *Province* columnist, I had no contract, except with the Devil who made me do it. In the editorial room, which I visited only once a week to deliver my copy to my editor, I was neither management nor labour. I had no place at either the boardroom table or the oil-barrel fire stoked by striking workers in the parking lot. I never had a designated parking place, with or without my name on it. In short, I had the tenure of a gadfly. And that dictated my hesitation to give a woman even a penetrating glance.

That was reason talking. Giving common sense an argument was my libido, which kept nagging me with reminders that stroking Captain Fracas, the family cat, although a tactile pleasure, did not entirely satisfy the sensual needs of a thirty-four-year-old man.

Hence my game plan: I would find a comely and intelligent young woman, establish that we were sexually compatible, get the nod from my mother and ask the lucky woman to marry me after we made a verbal premarital agreement that we would have no children or other dependents larger than a bread box.

Viewed from all angles, I saw this position as totally rational. I was being up-front with the paranoia inherent in a product of the Great Depression, a person who had witnessed his father scrambling desperately to support wife and child, and snatching at a donkey job that tethered him for life. I did not want to have to look at a child of *mine* as though he or she were to blame for my swallowing the anchor.

Selfish is the word that feminists apply to this male triumph of reason over the reproduction imperative. And they are right. A man—or, occasionally, a woman—*is* being selfish when he/she purposely eschews offspring in order to concentrate more fully on career. Einstein put it in writing to his wife: no kids, and sex by appointment only.

Genius doesn't do windows.

If I had had any sense in my iffy trade, I would have married a woman built like a boarding plank. It might have delayed procreation for at least a week or two. Instead, I married Myrl Heselton. Any objective judge would have

seen at a glance that this was a womanly woman, present-
ing dangerous curves that should have been signposted by
the highways department. Pathetic. I hear an echo of the
Wayne and Shuster sketch in which Wayne is bewitched by
one of the shapely women in the slave market: Shuster:
"Johnny, she's only a girl." Wayne: "I know, but she's so
good at it."

And Myrl could laugh. This can be a great comfort to a
humorist when the giggles extend beyond the rutting sea-
son. The compatibility was that of the pig farmer and the
woman he marries because she enjoys pork rinds, or of the
juggler wedded to someone whose hobby is mending bro-
ken plates.

For our honeymoon I took Myrl on a nine-month trip
around the world, the columns thus generated later appear-
ing as *Girdle Me a Globe*. Not mentioned in the book is the
event on that journey that struck terror into my tripes. Six
months into our safari, we stopped to rest our rented Fiat in
a small town in southern France. Myrl having felt unwell for
several weeks, I asked our innkeeper for a referral to the
local *médecin*. The doctor examined her, and a few days
later called us in to share his diagnosis.

"Le lapin est mort," he told us.

Being a former registrant at the Sorbonne, I had little dif-
ficulty in translating. "The rabbit died." So what? was my
initial reaction. Why were we referred to a vet?

Then I saw the doctor beaming and shaking my wife's
hand. The sou dropped. This quack had given Myrl a preg-
nancy test, and it had proved positive. The crashing sound I
heard was my world collapsing around me.

I wanted a second opinion. Second, third, fourth—as many
opinions as it would take to quash this first opinion. But I
could tell by the expression on Myrl's face that it wasn't

worth the trouble of finding another town, another doctor, another goddamn rabbit.

But I still couldn't believe it. I had carefully guided my wife for thousands of miles through the jungles of Ceylon and Araby's inspiringly barren desert, and in every kind of conveyance from Aussie banana boat to a camel in Karachi, without an accident. Now here was the Mother of All Misadventures. My marriage, indeed my whole life scenario, had been based on the premise that I was sterile, thanks to years of standing on my neck. Myrl and I had an oral premarital agreement that we would remain childless, because my being a newspaper columnist precluded any reproduction not approved by the pressmen's union.

My understanding of the agreement was that, in the unfortunate event of our becoming parents of a child, and

Shamelessly involving the kids—Christopher, Claire, Cathy—in some publicity shoot, c. 1966. Smile, damn you, smile!

divorce, we would split the child equally down the middle, dispose of the parts, and Mum's not the word.

Well, it didn't work out that way. The Life Force makes monkeys of us all. I couldn't blame that bottle of Chianti we drank in Rome for the arrivals of the two subsequent children. Catherine, Claire and Christopher Nicol were so named, in part, because their father, anticipating penury, wanted them to have initials that would favour their stealing monogrammed towels from Canadian National hotels. Today they are young adults, never charged.

The truth is, however, that being a family man provided me with Grade-A grist for the mill (*In Darkest Domestica*). Only when one weighs *all* the effects of child-rearing on one's career as a selfish bastard may one truthfully say: What we have between the ears is compromised by what we have between the legs.

On the other hand, as a way to build character, becoming a parent is probably preferable to serving in World War III.

Chapter 17

Bombing on Broadway

I n the late 1950s the two major events in Vancouver were the Coming of Marilyn Monroe—who convulsed Vancouver International Airport with a massive press conference, a scrum that called for more blockers than I could field—and the arrival of my daughter, Cathy, which mercifully drew a smaller crowd at St. Paul's Hospital.

When a pregnant Myrl and I arrived back in Vancouver, we found that my parents had rented a house for us to move into. They were in the process of selling their own home and moving to White Rock, possibly to forestall my moving back in with them one more time, with wife and infant. Crafty, my father. But I didn't begrudge them their freedom. They had given me their best shot as parents. Now it was time for them to move on to being grandparents, whom I looked forward to exploiting as much as possible.

Meanwhile my failing to have my photo taken sitting on Marilyn Monroe's lap provided further proof—if any were needed—that as an investigative reporter I didn't have the Write Stuff. I couldn't get an in-depth interview with my cleaning lady. I tried it with Mrs. Proski, but I never did find out why the coffee table was down to three legs.

So I had to assume I was better suited to creative writing. I was encouraged in this fantasy by my being hired by the creative writing department of UBC to teach, not implausibly, creative writing. Odd, that, since I was competent to instruct in all forms of creative writing except poetry, the short story, the novel, the Liberals' Red Book, the New Democratic Party Pink Book, the Progressive Conservatives' bank book, and graffiti.

It was Earle Birney, I think, who got me the job. Earle had a puckish sense of humour. Having upset the whole English department by creating the creative writing department, which made him the creator of creators, the charismatic poet created the part-time posts for marginally qualified writers like me so that he could buzz off in pursuit of the Muse. Birney was allergic to administration. He got into a nasty spat with Roy Daniells, the charming head of the English department and a fellow poet of great distinction. Both wanted the head's desk, but only Roy was prepared to sit behind it. As a friend of both men, I ate a lot of my lunches in the botanical garden to stay neutral.

These conflicts of empire building were savage enough to cow Caesar himself. To this stress was added the special intensity of creative writing students, who put a great deal of themselves into their work, and who sometimes cornered me in my office, as did the gorgeous, micro-minied blonde eager to explain why she had typed her poem in the form of

The Province *thought this skiing lesson might be funny (1958). Har-de-har. Writing can be painful.*

the female pubic area. (In that primitive era sexual harassment was known as "improving your grades.")

Creative writing teachers, I found, are subject to temptation like no other professional group except possibly psychiatrists. If I had had a couch in *my* office, I might have disgraced myself, and my alma mater, without ever really understanding the haiku.

After only a couple of semesters of the blind being led by the myopic, I retreated to the safety of my home study. To supplement the newspaper column, I launched into what I hoped would be literature, specifically a stage play with pretensions of significance. This venture might have proved more auspicious had I used another name, "Arthur Miller," for instance, or "Eugene O'Neill." Once a writer has been identified with serving up trifles, he aspires to the main dish at his peril.

Like Shakespeare—hey, nothing but the best—I went to history for my plot. The story that caught my eye was that of Regulus, the Roman general who, during the First Punic War, was captured by the Carthaginians and offered an alternative to his being tortured to death: his escorted return to Rome to persuade the Senate to sue for peace. Should he fail, Regulus would, on his word of honour, return to Carthage and submit to his execution.

Regulus agreed to the deal, went back to Rome, advised the Senate to continue the war, and returned to Carthage and a martyr's death. It was a great yarn and a glorious demonstration of personal integrity, not to mention a resonant object lesson for people in Ottawa, some of whom are not known for being prepared to die in order to keep their promise.

Regulus, the play, has a copious cast and enough scene changes to put a stage manager into shock therapy for years. Basically the play was unproduceable, something that was accepted as a challenge by Dorothy Davies, Vancouver's most dynamic and fearless stage director. I forget how she came by the script, but she persuaded the local chapter of the Voice of Women (VOW)—a prefeminist group of mostly upper-class, intellectual and antiwar women—that *Regulus* could serve as a fund-raiser. There was no money in the production for anyone else. A labour of love, it was, with the love waning as fast as the labour piled up.

Our venue was the Peretz School in Kerrisdale, where the rich folk live. The school had a small but gallant stage, with minimum facilities for flying any scenery except the author and, like the turkey, no wings for escape. I had written in so many characters that the cast members had to double, changing costumes behind a sheet backdrop of scenery that rippled throughout, as though Vesuvius were gearing up for an encore.

The cast, all volunteers, comprised the cream of Vancouver's thespian community. Among them were Robert Clothier (later Relic in CBC-TV's *The Beachcombers*), Peter Haworth, Shirley Broderick, Derek Ralston, and Norman Young, the godfather of Vancouver theatre to this day. Other cast members are now dead, though not, I like to believe, as a direct result of appearing in *Regulus*.

The remarkable thing about that one and only production of *Regulus* was that all the props and costumes were furnished by members of VOW from their own homes. We had a lot of lawn statuary from those stately manses, as well as Romanish vases, spears adapted from supernumerary golf clubs, and garbage can lids finding a new life as battle shields. Some of the togas, I gathered, were former wedding dresses, brought out of retirement for one last conquest.

On opening night, in the midst of delivering the prologue, Dorothy was startled to notice one of the pillars moving across the stage in the arms of its owner. A latecomer, the ambulant pillar was accepted by the audience as symbolic of something—there was a lot of Samuel Beckett and Bertolt Brecht going around at the time—and Dorothy pressed ahead as though confident that, given time, the pillar would settle down.

During many years of watching professional productions of my plays, I have never witnessed such concerned treatment of the props as that shown by our *Regulus* stagehands, all VOW members who had lent us their treasures. Nothing, absolutely nothing, was dropped on the floor, or banged in transit, or recklessly hustled during scene changes. The play had the majestic pace of a coronation at Westminster Abbey. Dorothy could flog the actors to shorten the evening, but was helpless to galvanize the crew backstage whose operative script was *Homes and Gardens*.

The play got mixed reviews: bad and worse. The audience of VOW supporters seemed to tolerate it, however, and the box office was bountiful. *Regulus* has never been done since. I blame the popularity of *A Funny Thing Happened on the Way to the Forum*, which totalled the toga drama for me and Charlton Heston.

This introduction to the hazards of live theatre did nothing to deter me from this form of self-immolation. With the sure instinct of the lemming, I rushed into writing what I conceived to be a contemporary comedy of manners—*Like Father, Like Fun*. Again the theme was integrity. A West Coast lumber tycoon bullies his public-relations man into procuring a girl to divert the tycoon's son from marrying on the green side of twenty. In his book *The Season: A Candid Look at Broadway (1967–68)*, William Goldman scrutinizes my play under the general classification "The Sex Comedy." That hurt. It was like calling William Congreve's *The Way of the World* a sex comedy, which it is, of course. But mine had redeeming features. These got lost somewhere between Vancouver's Playhouse Theatre and New York City's Brooks Atkinson. *Like Father, Like Fun* provides a clinical study of that holy grail of Canadian playwrights: the Broadway production.

Initially I tried to flog *Like Father* to both CBC Drama and UBC Theatre. Both threw their aprons over their heads, spooked by the play's use of voyeurism in the service of satire. I was about ready to consign the play to the bottom drawer—I have a desk consisting entirely of bottom drawers—when there came to town a new artistic director for the Vancouver Playhouse. His name was, and is, Malcolm Black. As a last hurrah, I left a copy of *Like Father* on his desk. A week later Malcolm phoned. He liked the play and wanted to include it in his 1966–67 season.

Here I must explain that Malcolm Black is a Liverpudlian. He had drunk from the same Pierian spring (the Mersey) as the Beatles. Some kind of magic must have invested Liverpool in the 1960s to diffuse irreverent talent upon a world gone stale. Malcolm not only took a chance on my glorified peep show but also put other homegrown BC playwrights—Paul St. Pierre and George Ryga—on the main stage and dared the culture snobs not to applaud.

Malcolm revelled in my play's somewhat prurient premise. He hired the most beautiful young actress in Canada, Pat Gage, to play the ingenue, and imported Ed McNamara, a master of the risibly uncouth, to portray the timber baron. The cast synthesized seamlessly under Malcolm's laid-back direction. Even our teenager, Reid Anderson, seconded from ballet school, showed the form that would later carry him to the top of Canada's ballet world. Despite the play's clumsy structure—a complete set change within the first act, a technical nightmare—the director spurred it along like a filly in open field.

The play was a hit. For the first, and probably last, time I heard the cries of "Author! Author!" from people outside my immediate family. The house sold out for the three-week run, and even the reviews acknowledged a phenomenon: an original Canadian play that presumed to be entertaining. The freak was noticed by Dave Broadfoot, a national institution

After the play gathering

IT WAS ONE BIG, EXCITING, SUCCESSFUL evening at the world premiere showing of Eric Nicol's comedy, "Like Father, Like Fun," and after the standing ovation, a delighted audience thronged into the upper lounge of the Playhouse to meet the author and players. A gooey, delicious cake in the shape of a stage, complete with marzipan actors, was presented to Mr. Nicol, left, and there to help him eat it were Mr. John G. Prentice, president of the board of directors of Playhouse Theatre Company, and Mrs. Prentice.

Enjoy it while it lasts, pal (1966). Fate waits outside with the custard pie poised. (UBC)

for lovers of comedy aimed north of the Forty-ninth parallel. Dave sent a signal to Ed Mirvish, the Toronto merchandiser-turned-impresario who had resurrected the Royal Alexandra Theatre. Mirvish booked our production into this *grande dame* of auditoria. Would the Fraser River start flowing east next? I wondered.

I did not go to Toronto for the opening night. A gut feeling, the kind that doesn't yield to Beano, told me the play was getting overextended. Mirvish had spared no expense in making the first night at the Royal Alex the most sensational opening since Moses parted the Red Sea. Bands played. The lieutenant governor of Ontario arrived in a horse-drawn carriage. Everyone who was anybody in Toronto, and a few who weren't, lavished formal wear on the lobby, while the theatre critics, ranged at the bar, sharpened their teeth for this prize prey. Among these was the highly corrosive Nathan Cohen, who had created a national reputation for himself as the enfant terrible of Canadian drama criticism. A rotund figure, he affected the slouch hat, black cape and sword cane that were the panoply of George Jean Nathan, the 1920s New York theatre critic responsible for the high suicide rate among Broadway play producers. Like his exemplar, everything that Cohen touched turned to gored.

As reported back to me by Malcolm on the phone, these first-night extravagances, conveyed to our Vancouver cast in their dressing rooms, created near-hysteria in one or two actors who up to then had played their roles without losing contact with the stage, but were now ready to close the gap between characterization and hyperventilating.

In short, all the factors were in place for our hyped-up Humpty-Dumpty to be served as a western-style omelette. Which it was, by the critics at least. Once the pressure was off, however, subsequent audiences carried the play for several months, in tandem with the Second City Revue. The production moved on to Montreal, where it was easier to meet expectations for a play written by an Anglo, and Mirvish decided to take the play to Broadway.

At the time this evolvement struck me as being an unexpected bonus, like dying and going to Heaven. Sure, it

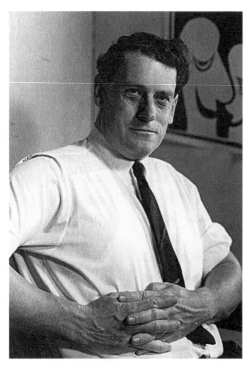

The poster boy ruminates, c. 1965:
"Is there film in that camera?" (UBC)

meant I had to join the Dramatists Guild of America, in company with Neil Simon and James Thurber. But I had never been strongly anti-union. Jimmy Hoffa had his good points.

I also acquired an agent—William Morris of New York City—to draw up my contract. I studied it carefully, and found no clause stating that, in the event of the play's folding early, I would be required to clean up Central Park with a blunt stick for the rest of my natural life.

It all looked good to me. The first cloud to appear on the eastern horizon was US labour law that demanded that *Like Father, Like Fun* have an entirely new, made-in-Manhattan production. New director, new cast, new set design, new everything except the author, who just needed renovation. The new director was flown out to Vancouver from New York to point out to me the parts of the play—all of it, actually—that required elective surgery. Unlike Malcolm Black, who was masculine with no additives, the new director was, shall we say, a tad precious. We were not on the same wavelength, my wave being less limp. However, the man's credentials being superior to mine, I dutifully rewrote whole scenes to remove the West Coast bark chips. I didn't trust my own judgement—even more damaging than not trusting one's spouse.

The second hint that both I and Abraham Lincoln should have stayed out of the theatre: a title search revealed that *Like Father, Like Fun* had already been used by an American author of mystery novels. To avoid the awful fury of copyright law, I was instructed to find a new title. This was like renaming an only child. The mind fights it to the death. What finally lay on the bier—*A Minor Adjustment*—was not borne proudly to the theatre marquee. I cursed it, and have never read an American mystery novel since.

The third evil omen: the producer's choice for the lead in the play, comedian Don Rickles, withdrew. Possessing all the charm of a snapping turtle, Rickles was ideal for the part. He was replaced by Austin Willis, a nice man, but completely wrong for the role.

I therefore arrived in New York City braced for the worst. The city did not disappoint me. In fact, it was fascinating, in a cobralike sort of way, to observe how the New York media and theatre people viewed this Canadian play that had wandered out of the north woods and somehow got corralled in one of Broadway's most prestigious theatres. They made no effort to disguise their opinion that we had missed a street sign, that we should be on the boards at Madison Square Garden, not the Brooks Atkinson, which would show the blood.

My lodging was the Algonquin Hotel, scene of the legendary Round Table whose bibulous knights were Dorothy Parker, Robert Benchley and Alexander Woollcott—the jousting jesters who in the 1920s made the *New Yorker* the Camelot of humour. Forty years later the Algonquin had grown senile. Residents still took bows when leaving the elevator, but all was rheumatic. I had hoped, simply by breathing, to inhale wit, if not wisdom. All I got was the diesel exhaust of garbage trucks greeting the dawn. One day in the mouldering lounge I did encounter Peter Ustinov. He looked no more inspirited than I felt. His play, *Halfway Up the Tree*, followed mine into the Brooks Atkinson and lasted only a few days longer.

My first meeting with my director was even more disillusioning. I found him living in a bed-sitter above a dry cleaner. His first inquiry was "Can I borrow twenty bucks?"

Hovering in the background was a large black lady whose frosty stare spoke volumes about the urgency of reimbursement for cleaning the place. In a matter of seconds I was out US$20, and we hadn't even started rehearsals. At this rate, my being paid for travel and hotel expenses, plus a generous per diem, could be quickly eroded. I was glad the play didn't have a large cast. *Show Boat* could have killed me.

To conserve my financial gains and avoid the horror unfolding at the play's rehearsals, I spent most of my weeks in town either sight-seeing—New York has two sights: the Statue of Liberty and the Brooklyn Bridge—or in my hotel room making notes for a book about the burgeoning calamity across Times Square (*A Scar Is Born*). At one point I was moved enough by the doomed proceedings on our stage to interject a criticism, voiced to the director during a break in the disaster: "This thing looks like amateur night in Hoboken."

The director flew into a rage. "It is *not* amateur night in Hoboken!" He might have even stamped his foot. "You don't know *anything* about theatre!"

Then he burst into tears. Now, back in Vancouver, Malcolm had never cried during rehearsal. And I had never before made a man weep, in any circumstances. I regretted my outburst. Maybe I *had* spent too much time in a

Roy Peterson's priceless poster, 1968. He catches the inner me.

Vancouver Island logging camp. Jeez, was I a bully?

No, I was a coward. I did not attend the opening night of my play on Broadway. Having to rent a tuxedo was only part of my avoiding the crucifixion, which included the post-mortal party atop 999, the traditional way of reducing the review-riddled playwright to rubble. I delegated Myrl to sit in for me, while I sat in a bar down the street, nursing a brandy. When she returned, I could tell by her expression that we would be catching the first northbound train out of town.

Desolate because my play had defecated on the Canada-wide expectation that the Broadway production had elicited, I sought anonymity in the crowds of Montreal's Expo 67. Canada was 100 years old, the same age I felt.

All in all, I have to disagree with Frank Sinatra: New York City is not all it's cracked up to be—the sidewalks excepted. (P.S. I never got my twenty bucks back.)

Chapter 18

Did I Miss Something?

H e who writes and runs away lives to write another play. Several plays, in fact. I was encouraged by Vancouver Playhouse director Malcolm Black who, being English, was not impressed by New York's rejection of *Like Father*. If a playwright can't have a Québécois director, a Brit will do nicely. Left to my own Canadian inferiority complex, I would have noticed that my head had been cut off, in New York, and brooded about it.

Nor was Joy Coghill, the irrepressible artistic director of Vancouver's Holiday Theatre, deterred from producing my children's plays (*Beware the Quickly Who*, *The Clam Made a Face*), which are still being done in stock. Eat your heart out, Broadway.

Still, I had learned that American acceptance is *the* criterion of judgement of Canadian stage plays, books, films, the lot. If Jesus chose Canada for the Second Coming, and performed miracles as convincing as the first time around, there would yet be Canadians who would say, "If you're the Messiah, how come you aren't working in the States?"

In the 1960s it was much easier to be a Canadian playwright and still eat than it is in the 1990s. The country was flush. A theatre company needed only to hold out a hand, and unless the fingernails were really dirty, some govern-

Lorraine McAllister was in the same show, but had better legs than Horton. (UBC)

ment would cross its palm with silver, even folding money.

A good example was *The Canadian Centennial Play*. This opus—now memorable to no one, including those of us on the committee that wrote it—was a federal project, part of the general celebration of the country's remaining intact for 100 years. (Today Ottawa distributes a few flags for Canada Day and prays that the one-man pipe band can play big.)

To write *The Centennial Play*, the federal government commissioned a number of Canadian playwrights whose names, if not household words, were at least known to Revenue Canada. Besides me, summoned to the capital to discuss the collaboration on this theatrical tribute to national cohesion were such dramatic eminences as W.O. Mitchell, Gratien Gélinas and a couple of other immortals whose names evade me.

We were gathered around a table, I remember, as cordial as a gaggle of tomcats. Ringmaster for this menagerie of egos was Nicholas Goldschmidt, who had a reputation for producing expensive international festivals despite all efforts to stop him.

Goldschmidt's initial concept—that we playwrights work together in the collegial if testy manner of Gilbert and Sullivan—was quickly deep-sixed. We didn't trust each other in the vicinity of our reputations, nor any farther than we could throw the Peace Tower. We were unanimous in agreeing that, although multiple paternity may have worked for the Fathers of Confederation, it was bad breeding for a radio play. As a junior partner in this doomed enterprise, I was deeply impressed by the expertise of my more distinguished colleagues in sharing nothing but the federal largesse.

Bidding a rather wan Goldschmidt goodbye, each of us dramatists returned to his own part of this vast land of ours, grateful for the distance between us and the nation's capital, and greatly enriched. Not culturally. Just enriched.

I wouldn't go as far as to say that the seeds of separatism were sown by *The Centennial Play*. It probably should not be linked to Pierre Trudeau's having to invoke the War Measures Act to subdue violence in Quebec in 1970. On the other hand, production of the play was never repeated. The script likely lies in a file of the Canadian Security Intelligence Service with other subversive material.

Other extravagances of that annus mirabilis, 1967, have survived better. The Centennial Flame, unlike our play, was not promptly extinguished, but has guttered on. Likewise the National Arts Centre, built in Ottawa as the showpiece of Canada's performing arts, has remained as a monument to the sacrifice of taxpayers' money.

In fact, the NAC was still standing in 1972 when a stage play of mine, *Pillar of Sand*, had its premiere there, drawing notices that glowed only after I set fire to them. I should have known that the omens were on the dire side. First, I received an opening-night wire from Pierre Trudeau, wishing me luck. It is part of Canadian theatre superstition that to get a good-luck telegram from a reigning prime minister is the French kiss of death. Also, I didn't see Pierre in the throng of formally dressed diplomats, bureaucrats and other prats, an international audience guaranteed to miss any mes-

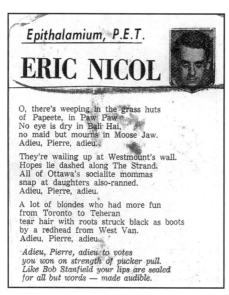

Epithalamium, P.E.T.

ERIC NICOL

O, there's weeping in the grass huts
of Papeete, in Paw Paw
No eye is dry in Bali Hai,
no maid but mourns in Moose Jaw.
Adieu, Pierre, adieu.

They're wailing up at Westmount's wall.
Hopes lie dashed along The Strand.
All of Ottawa's socialite mommas
snap at daughters also-ranned.
Adieu, Pierre, adieu.

A lot of blondes who had more fun
from Toronto to Teheran
tear hair with roots struck black as boots
by a redhead from West Van.
Adieu, Pierre, adieu.

*Adieu, Pierre, adieu to votes
you won on strength of pucker pull.
Like Bob Stanfield your lips are sealed
for all but words — made audible.*

We also do lite verse when the occasion (Pierre's wedding, 1971) inspires. (UBC)

An unfunny thing happened on the way to the Ottawa forum, 1972.
The National Arts Centre is the playwright's Death Valley.

With Edward Everett Horton, plugging a Vancouver production of
The Front Page, *c. 1963.*

sage not delivered in a pouch.

Second, on a kiosk outside the NAC I noticed a poster hyping the play as sponsored by du Maurier. At the bottom of the poster was Warning: Smoking May Be Hazardous to Your Health.

I felt sick about writing a play aimed at the heart and hitting only the lungs. Plainly I would have been more benignly occupied selling aluminum siding to homeless widows.

After *Pillar of Sand* died—coughing horribly—I swore I

would never again accept sponsorship by a tobacco company or a Trudeau government. This crisis of conscience has continued to harass the arts community in Canada. It is no fun being a produced playwright, or a concert pianist, or a prima ballerina, if the letters in your alphabet soup keep forming Mea Culpa. A person could choke.

Do bad reviews hurt? For your stage play, your book, your new hairdo, whatever? You bet they do. The gestation period for a two-act play, or a 300-page novel, is the same as for a human baby: about nine months. The big difference is, when the maternity nurse hands you the newborn child, she doesn't say, "Wow, *that's* an ugly little bastard."

The parent can be happy with his or her baby, despite its looking like a gargoyle fallen off a medieval church, whereas a scathing review of your artistic work slits your self-esteem up a treat. In contrast, instant success and fame take longer to destroy you.

I was able to survive the massive and repeated shrapnel of egg on my face because I never put all my eggs in one basket. With morale sustained by the readership of a now-syndicated newspaper column, I could write plays for the fun and challenge of the medium, like chess, only with live pieces on the boards.

Writing is like other types of investment: an author should diversify, with a portfolio of low-interest-bearing works (for academic journals) blended with sex novels written from the point of view of the vibrator. The downside of protecting your megalomania this way is that you risk never becoming especially famous for anything. Thus my entry in *The Canadian Encyclopedia* refers to me as "a jack of all trades," the implication being that I have been the master, or mistress, of none. The trouble with this assessment is that it is accurate. It would have been nicer had the citation called me "an all-rounder," or "a true Renaissance man." But, of course, one can't expect an extensive work like an encyclopedia to catch all the nuances.

The point is, despite getting my lumps from theatre critics from Broadway to Burnaby, I continued to write stage plays, which found me new avenues to trouble. Like *Ma!* This adventure began with an idea in the mind of one of Canada's liveliest actresses-directors, Joy Coghill: that she would play the role of Margaret ("Ma") Murray in a play that showcased the career of the newspaper editor who made "and that's fur damshur" the most quoted judgement in a half-century of BC politics.

Myself, I had never particularly admired Ma Murray. A public scold—that was my opinion of the Oracle of Lillooet. I probably envied the veneration in which she was held by the metropolitan press, whose editorials had to be modulated to a degree of civility. And the power that Ma wielded—tongue-lashing the premier, W.A.C. Bennett, whenever his government strayed from the gospel according to St. Margaret—presaged the coming of feminist clout.

However, I took the assignment to write the play, essentially as a vehicle for Joy. She was, and I believe still is, a friend from university days, and I knew she would be sensational in the role, regardless of whether the vehicle had square wheels. The only qualm I had came from writing a comedy/drama whose central character was not only a real person but still alive. Having been once sued for libel, and lost, I had no desire to become a repeat offender. When you have seen one lawyer for the plaintiff, you've seen them all. They share that smug look of the predator that has its prey by the short hairs.

I therefore concentrated my research on talking to Ma Murray's daughter, Georgina Keddell, repeatedly seeking

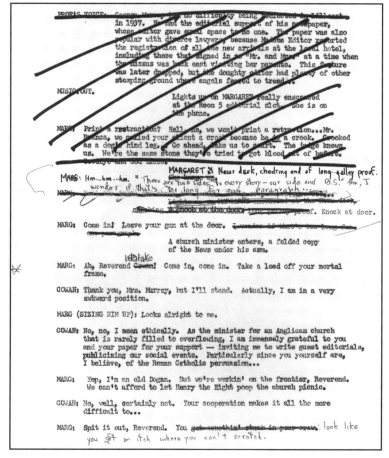

A page from the production script of Ma!, *1981. If at first you don't succeed, try playwriting. Life becomes an extended revision. (UBC)*

assurance that the firebrand had died down to a clinker, inert and harmless in her nineties. I would have preferred to see a death certificate, signed by a reputable doctor, but I didn't want to seem pushy.

I also put trust in the fact that the play's coproducer was the CBC, whose regional director, Len Lauk, impressed me as unlikely to wager public money on the dramatized biography

233

A hit, or at least a glancing blow, 1981. This vehicle for Joy Coghill really had wheels.

of someone whose breathing passed the mirror test. Little did I know that Len had a puckish sense of humour that totally unfitted him for an executive position in the Mother Corp. He departed from Herself shortly after helping me into the glue.

Under these eminent auspices the premiere of *Ma!* was an Event. After the Broadway debacle of *Like Father, Like Fun*, my policy had been to avoid any event, short of my own funeral. I preferred occasions to be low-key, audible only to bullfrogs.

The chosen city for *this* event was Kamloops. I had hoped that our opening in Kamloops would be regarded as the out-of-town tryout, in the tradition of Broadway-bound shows previewed in New Haven, Connecticut. But Kamloops would have none of it. The town made available the largest theatre it could offer: the vast, echoing Sagebrush, an adjunct of the major high school. When I saw it, my heart sank like a stone. The tiers of seats—of the functional type made to have school lunches spilled on them—rose in row after row, balcony upon balcony, every seat in the gods and a nose-bleed with your program.

A school auditorium on steroids—that was the venue for *Ma!* From bitter experience I knew that, in a house of more than 1,000 seats, the only stage production with a hope in theatrical hell is spectacle, something mounted by Andrew Lloyd Whatsit. And my playscript for *Ma!* did not include a chandelier crashing to the floor. The only thing set to fall was my face.

The Nicol Law of Theatre Dimensions is basic: one cannot do intimate theatre in the Hollywood Bowl. The audience in the upper balcony *must* be close enough to enjoy without binoculars the cleavage of ladies in the orchestra seats. How else does the playwright's work weather the draggy bits, as when the male lead swallows a fly?

Even Shakespeare would have found it tough going if his plays had been done at the Ford Centre for the Performing Arts instead of the cozy Globe. And *Ma!* offered nothing like a covey of chorus girls costumed as alley cats, slithering out of a million dollars' worth of steamy scenery.

So I pleaded with the custodian of the Sagebrush to at least partition off the upper reaches, as was permitted by an enormous accordion variant on the Berlin Wall. No joy. The management was confident of filling the entire house with paying customers, regardless of my fate when the gag lines were heard only by patrons equipped with sonar.

One of the most difficult roles in theatre is for the playwright to look confident and buoyant on opening night when in his heart he knows he is about to suffer two hours of such exquisite torture as would draw a gasp from the Iron Maiden. For this he dresses in his best suit, anticipating the casket on which will be tossed a bouquet of deadly nightshade.

But *Ma!* was to add terror to trepidation. As the first-nighters were milling around in the lobby, I saw come through the door a wheelchair in which sat a very old lady whom I recognized at once. Ma Murray! Not only alive but escorted by a couple of tall, muscular young men—her grandnephews, I learned later—easily large enough to lead the lynching.

Ma was immediately surrounded by an admiring throng. She accepted the adulation deadpan, an expression that could have indicated advanced senility or a mask for carrying a gun. Her escort wheeled her to a place of honour, dead centre, first balcony, as close to a royal box as the Sagebrush could manage without a major renovation. The seats around Ma were filled by her followers, chatting convivially in a scene redolent of the emperor's court in Rome's Colosseum, waiting for the first Christian to be thrown to the lions.

The Moment came in the opening scene of Act 2. It was one of the rare poignant scenes of the play, with Ma and husband George Murray alone on the stage discussing their relationship. In the sobered silence of the audience, a voice suddenly cawed from the brow of the balcony, "Who are those people and what are they doing?"

It was Ma, in full throat of her senile dementia. The house responded with a roar of laughter that topped everything evoked by my script, as written. A real showstopper, her line was, freezing the actors and dropping a lead balloon into my gut. The play staggered to its conclusion with further asides from the gratuitous Voice Off, and ended to tumultuous applause. For what, or whom, who could say? All I knew for sure was that, when the house lights went up, most of the audience was looking at Ma Murray, the cynosure of a standing ovation. If someone was shouting "Author! Author!" my voice was drowned out by the accolade directed elsewhere.

Backstage, scene of the postperformance party, I got buffeted by people pushing through to shake the hand of the wrinkled icon slouched in the wheelchair. Eventually someone introduced me to her. My name was obviously unfamiliar, but her wheelchair greeted my foot. Ma then launched into a speech that indicated she thought she was haranguing the Cattlemen's Association. She rambled on at length, deploring the price of beef and the dereliction of the provincial government in failing to support the ranchers of the Interior.

The party was still rocking when I stole away to my solitary hotel room. First Broadway, now Kamloops. Playwriting can be a bummer—and that's fur damshur.

Chapter 19

A Serving of Hard Cheese

Baby boomers, I hear, are having a bit of a problem explaining to their children why they shouldn't do drugs—the pot calling the kettle. The parents must either accept their children's toking up as a harmless rite of juvenile passage, or concede their own brain damage, which qualifies them to lecture no family member but the cat.

But aside from losing all credibility with their kids, the pioneers of permissivism remember the 1960s and 1970s with nostalgia. I do not. As a source of sentimental yearning, those decades are right up there with the Black Death and a root canal.

The sexual revolution found me on the side of the ancien régime. I witnessed my children getting a prescription from that patent quack, Dr. Timothy Leary—"Tune in, turn on, drop out"—and knew that medicare would never cover it.

Dr. Leary's ashes were recently rocketed into space as a warning to aliens thinking of experimenting with drugs. I would have liked to have seen him leave earlier. Yes, my three children, then teenagers, all got into trouble of various popular styles. I blamed the rock concerts.

Gift of love

ERIC NICOL

For the opening night of a play of mine, members of the company presented me with a necklace of love beads. I didn't wear them, because they didn't go with the albatross.

Actually I'm not too sure what it means to wear love beads. Do they signal the intention of loving, or a desire to be loved? Or is the loving betokened by love beads the more general love of mankind, as with the man who loved humanity but couldn't stand people?

I don't frequent the flower people enough to be au courant about love beads. As a non-smoker I can see their usefulness as something with which to occupy one's hands, but a socially nervous person like myself could conceivably twist them into a rather nasty case of auto-garrote.

Writing for the stage involves human contact. Scary, but it does make you more aware of clothes (1968). (UBC)

And myself, for being a workaholic—possibly the worst kind of addiction for a parent. I should have spent more time with my kids than did the Rolling Stones.

Holidays are for losers. That was my mantra. The more my wife and adolescent children found other companions to have fun with, the further I buried myself in my work. I had forgotten, from my own childhood, how important it is for a father to accompany his children on summer vacations at campground or cottage. The family that suffers together has the better chance of sticking together. And just paying the tab doesn't cover the bill.

After my daughters left home for lovers, and wife Myrl found less incentive to put up with the aging beaver up in the study, I was left with a preteen son. Desperate to save something of my family, I got Chris into the Air Cadets and dutifully ferried him to the drill hangar, applauding his marching skills, buffing his service boots. Then, at graduation, he won the squadron lottery: an all-expenses-paid trip for two to Fiji.

Instead of going with him (I'd seen Fiji) I drafted his seventeen-year-old sister Claire as chaperone. More bad judgement. My two younger children returned from the South Pacific paradise with that satisfied look of the cat that ate the yah-yah bird. Chris never wore the uniform again.

It was not long afterward that my son left home and school to join a rock band as a guitarist, and plumb the depths of fashionable degradation.

However, all my now-aged-thirtyish kids are recovered from that rite of passage. We are on good terms that I credit to my never having abandoned them to their folly. Their mother, too, to her credit, kept the light in the window of where she now lived.

A bit of advice to young parents: Never slam the door against the prodigal son or daughter. You may catch your fingers.

These family problems were for me no stimulus to writing humour. The typewriter becomes a place to lay your

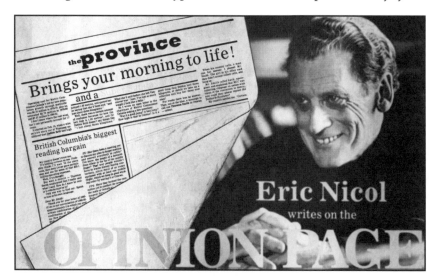

Apparently I had an opinion, but I don't care for that leer (c. 1960).

head and have a good cry. For troubles, when they come, arrive as a convention. There are periods in the life of the funnyman when it would be more practical to work as a poet or a plumber.

My parents were dying. In the process Pop became an extended-care patient in White Rock Hospital. Initially he enjoyed the attention he got, sitting in his wheelchair in the lobby, wearing his Legion jacket and beret, selling poppies on Remembrance Day and flirting with the nurses. A trouper to the end. My mother, though, had withdrawn into the polite, inscrutable silence of arteriosclerosis in a nursing home I hated almost as much as myself.

I managed to find a retirement home for them to share in Ladner, British Columbia—closer to my place—and with the help of their grandson moved them into this last promising address. The second day there, my father, using his cane, slipped in a pool of my incontinent mother's urine. Hip broken, after a failed operation, he died. Mom had had the last word, without one.

My mother completed her days peacefully at St. Vincent's Nursing Home in Vancouver, where I could wheel her through the pleasant gardens until the night she gave up the Irish ghost.

Too late, I acknowledge the debt I owe them. To my father, the delight in eliciting laughter. If there is such a thing as a humour gene, I got mine from Pop.

To my mother, I owe the transfusion of lively language as she peppered her small talk with Irish spices…

On weak beverage: "It's water bewitched and tea begrudged."

On dry mouth: "I couldn't spit sixpence."

On criticism: "He did her a drop o' no good."

On a forbidding sky: "Black as Newgate's knocker."

Hey, look at all them books! I must read one of 'em some time (1978).

And *the* euphemistic curse: "Godfrey Daniel Simpson Smith's Blasting Ironworks!"

Mom was my first proofreader. If she laughed at my column, it went to the newspaper. If she didn't, I junked it. Her comic taste was impeccable.

A little late, here, folks, but—thanks for the gift of motley.

A chicken in every pot, and pot in every chick. Long hair and short attention spans. Free love. Do not pay for sex until 1999! Oh, I could have had it all.

I, too, could have been one of those writers—proliferative in that permissive age—who lived it up so that they could write it down. If I had not been so hooked on antique principles, I might have been invited to join that exclusive eastern club of authors and publishers who got together regularly to drink, sing bawdy songs and have sex with strippers. What a waste of my life! Virtue is its own reward? Not in paperback. Hell, I've since learned that there were Catholic priests in that era who were having more fun than I was.

Who wants to read stuff written by a person who has never smoked anything, who has spurned both beer and booze, has been faithful to his spouse, has never been arrested for crime, or been a Conservative prime minister?

Determined to expose myself to at least one weekend of temptation and make one last, desperate stab at profligacy, I flew alone to Las Vegas. But temptation failed to notice me. After losing $10 on the slots,

I must have been trying to sell something when this photo was taken, but I forget what, and when (possibly Second Dynasty). (UBC)

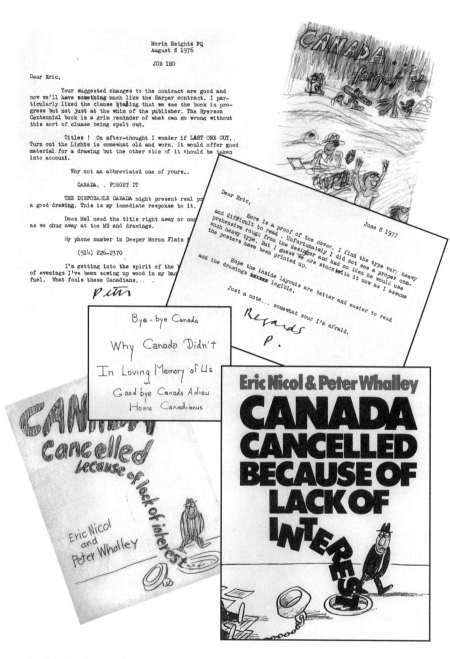

The birth of a book title, Peter Whalley assisting, without anaesthetic. (UBC)

and finding that hookers declined to be picked up by some-
one riding a bicycle, I flew home with character unchanged
from that of someone out of *Anne of Green Gables*.

Soon after, amid my family crises, some of my angst
broke into unsightly print with the publication of *Letters to
My Son*, an update of Lord Chesterfield's advice to his way-
ward scion. Some reviewers expressed shock. Although life
is a box of chocolates according to Forrest Gump, what they
expected to get from me was a soft centre. Instead they bit
into a sourball. There were reports that some older female
fans had a fit of the vapours upon encountering explicit sex
under the covers of this book.

I felt badly about this. I had violated one of the first rules
of surviving as a writer: continue to give your readers what
they have learned to expect from you. If you are Stephen
King, you give them horror, book after book. Margaret
Atwood, feminist turmoil. Farley Mowat, a torrid love affair
with wolves, whales, whatever the Maritimers are slaugh-
tering as a surrogate for having a team in the National
Hockey League.

The royalty statements for *Letters to My Son* cured me of
this aberration without prescription drugs. And my morale
was restored when publisher Mel Hurtig sent me a manu-
script of funny drawings entitled "The Joy of Hockey" by
Alberta artist David More. Mel wanted text to go with the
merry pictures. Never having played hockey, or even learned
to skate, I readily accepted the challenge. To date, *The Joy of
Hockey* has sold more than 30,000 copies and spawned a
successful series of sports books—*The Joy of Football*,
Tennis: It Serves You Right, *Golf: The Agony and the Ecstasy*,
Skiing Is Believing—subjects about which my ignorance was
virtually total.

Conclusion: in Canada books on sports are the only serious

```
              Lecture #9 -- Satiric, Light Verse & Irony

                        be
1.  Non-lyrical verse may of a fair number of different kinds.   Often

    lumped together under the general term "satiric verse".  But satire
                                              Blasted Pine, VII
    is a much-abused word in poetry as it is in prose.  For instance, Dryden

    is usually described as being a master of satiric verse, but much of

    the satire is very clever lampooning in that it is directed against an

    individual rather than a larger condition of society.  Thus, though

    Dryden's reputation remains high, nobody but English specialists read   some of

    his so-called satiric poems.  (E.g. "Mac Flecknoe", Dryden's Poetical

    Works, p. 150)  Notable for use of rhymed couplets, and incisiveness

    of language, which set a pattern for this type of poetry for that is

    still being adopted. The personal vendetta is the most perishable type

    of material for satiric verse.  The smaller the target, the smaller the

    poem, and the smaller the chances of its survival.  Pope, in
                     castigated                    Blasted Pine IV
    the Dunciad, mocked bad poets.  Another e.g. (Intro to Lit.,

    p. 398), but (quiz) presents the larger picture of country vs. city

    life.  Has a social as well as personal and individual interest.

    Contemporary example of lampooning individual, and through him a

    state of larger affairs:"W.L.M.K." in The Blasted Pine, p. 27  .

    Difference between this and personification of object of satire:

    "Canada: Case History" by Birney (op. cit., p 3 ).  Discuss Layton's

    "Colony to Nation" (loc. cit.)  Didactic function of verse.

    -- further example of role of rhyme, contrasted with unrhymed lyrical

    verse: "Two Goodbyes for Charlie" (Prism, Summer '64)

    Satire on a whole era: T.S. Eliot's "Prufrock"  (Intro to Lit., p. 421)

    Mixture of beauty and banality, of recondite words and simple phrasing.

    Verbal shifts.  Poetry of discord.  Satirizing modern man through

    an imaginary individual.  Dilettante, inhibited, unltra-fastiduous.

    Can give himself to art but not to life! Dare not risk a decision.
    Note use of rhyme, but with much variation in metre of lines.  Subtle rhythm.
```

*Instructor's notes for creative writing, University of BC, 1964.
Teaching, I found, is much tougher than producing what teachers
teach. It's theatre without help from scenery. (UBC)*

contenders with the Bible as guaranteed bestsellers. This country's best and funniest sportswriter, Jim Taylor, did for Wayne Gretzky what the New Testament did for Christ, namely, pushed other biographies off the charts.

Buoyed by the success of the sports books, I was ready for a new relationship with someone who would enrich my celibate existence. My bank manager introduced me to a broker. It was lust at first sight. Clark Macdonald seduced me away from my fidelity to my stamp collection as my main hedge against inflation, poverty in old age and economy-class cremation. The experience taught me that a person may be casual about choosing a marriage partner, but selecting the right broker is *the* way to get a good night's sleep.

Mine helped me reach my financial goal of being a millionaire by age sixty-five—with six months to spare. Just as well. Have you priced mousetrap cheese lately?

Already indebted to UBC for the first chance to get my nonsense published, I had that institution to thank for introducing me to the woman who became my new wife. Mary Razzell was a mature student in English, whose department ran a short-story contest for which I acted as one of the judges. Mary's story won second prize, and at the celebratory luncheon we met over a crusty roll.

Mary later phoned to invite me to join her at a campus reading of Irish poetry. Talk about your mixed emotions! Here was the first time a woman—and a gorgeous one at that—had asked me for a date in living memory. But it was for an evening of Irish verse. Read at me, verse whether Irish or peaceable makes me comatose. I experienced several seconds of inner conflict before asking for a Celtic rain check.

Later, after getting a second opinion from my gonads, I phoned Mary and told her bluntly, "I'd like very much to meet you for lunch, unless your interest is in my helping

Collaborator Dave More, heavily disguised (right), *shares responsibility for* Tennis-It Serves You Right, *1984.*

you find a publisher for a novel you've written."

"It isn't," Mary said. "I want you for your body."

Bingo! The correct answer! Give that lady the thousand-dollar bedroom suite.

I knew that Mary didn't mean it. She had never seen my body below a university dining room table. But it was the thought that counted.

Mary, also separated, and also with three grown-up children, meant common interests in chaos. I was absolutely enchanted to squire a beautiful woman who was eager to further her education and writing talent, and who was—the clincher—a registered nurse. For this middle-aged man, what a treasure! To hell with Francis Bacon's "Wives are young men's mistresses, companions for middle age, and old men's nurses!" I would cover all three generations of wife with one vivacious brunette.

Author Mary Razzell (five young-adult novels) and husband, 1995. Russell Kelly photo (BCBW)

We were married on February 11, 1986. Since then Mary has become one of Canada's leading authors of young-adult fiction, with five published novels under her twenty-six-inch belt.

As for me, I've retired from the bench as a writing contest judge. I guess I know when to quit while I'm ahead.

Mary helped me with the research for the last major mistake of my writing career. I had got a phone call from Douglas Gibson, an old friend and the peerless editor who had piloted me through *Vancouver*—a successful history of

the city—and several other books which, against my reli-
gion, involved work. Doug mentioned that he had discov-
ered that one of Charles Dickens's sons, Francis, had served
in the North-West Mounted Police. Maybe there was a novel
to be found in the dodgy tour of duty of this gaffe-prone
progeny who was dubbed "Chickenstalker" by his father.

I bit. And after a year of scarifying research, the novel
was written as a series of Frank's letters to acquaintances in
England, describing his foul-ups, some true, others ficti-
tious. *Dickens of the Mounted* was published as a hoax. Why
Doug Gibson let me convince him that this would be a bit
of a lark, God knows and the Devil suspects. Sometimes a
kind of madness overtakes authors who have done more
research and breathed more library dust than their systems
can tolerate.

We even implicated the normally prudent archivist of the
University of British Columbia, George Brandak, who agreed
to have his photo taken with me in Special Collections, por-
ing over yellowed documents alleged to be Frank Dickens's
letters but, as I recall, were actually old laundry lists pre-
pared by early Union Steamships. Oh, yes, when I dig my
own grave I leave room for other bodies.

The book's dust jacket identified me as the "editor" of
Frank's letters, not the author of a novel. People bought and
read the book, believing that the letters were authentic—a not
unreasonable assumption, considering the amount of trouble
I had gone to validating historical background. I had planted
one clue, a letter in which Dickens describes meeting Colonel
Flashman, the rakish hero of *The Flashman Papers*, "edited"
by George MacDonald Fraser with happier result than *my*
fooling with the bogus. No one noticed the clue.

Right away the fecal matter hit the fan. A couple of book
reviewers got sucked in, guaranteeing that no work of mine

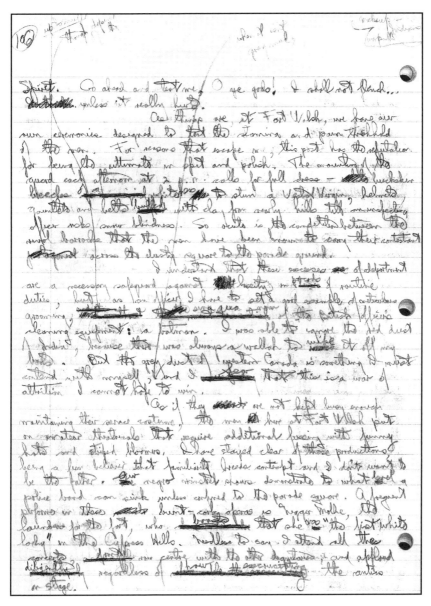

Chicken tracks from first draft of Dickens of the Mounted, *1989. For me, composing on typewriter or computer is like kissing through chicken wire: sensually incomplete.*

would ever win their approval again. A number of readers tried to return their copies to booksellers, demanding a refund even though they had received the book as a gift. At least one university professor of Canadian history went public with his praise of the petard on which he was promptly hoisted and, worst of all, an officer high in Ottawa's RCMP command stamped the book with his imprimatur as the most accurate account of that period of North-West Mounted Police history.

Archivist Brandak—who has, I believe, dyed his hair and unlisted his phone number—still gets letters from around the world from academics and Dickens clubs asking for confirmation that *Dickens of the Mounted* comprises bona fide epistles.

As for sales of the book, they indicate that God punishes humbuggers. Oh, what a tangled web we weave when first we practise to deceive! Or at least I needed a lot more practice.

Chapter 20

In the Wake of Willy Loman

What I try to get over is the fact that I've published more than thirty books. It wasn't the writing that took a lot out of me. Writing is agony, of course, but usually the twitch in the eye, the plucking at the coverlet, subside after a few months of psychiatric counselling. What the published author *never* recovers from—may, in fact, be identified by the coroner as the actual cause of death—is the promotional tour.

Rule of thumb: the larger the author's advance on royalties, the more intensive the promotional tour. Any advance over $50,000 pretty well dictates your reserving a bed at the Mayo Clinic. Many contracts now bind the author into an extended promotional tour, the biggest setback for personal freedom since the Portuguese slave ships.

Here I must inject a modifier. There *are* authors who not only survive their book promotion tours but profess to enjoy them. Pierre Berton is an example of this hardy breed. Berton was bred in the Yukon and has the toughness of a sled dog, the quality needed by the writer who is mushed from city to city in a time that minimizes the cost of hotel bills. Pierre, I understand, can be run for days without pause to pee or poop.

None of my books has been prestigious enough to warrant an international promotion tour, such as that inflicted on disgraced members of the British royal family. But even a Canadian tour of populated centres west of Quebec can, I've found, suffice to guarantee the writer's return home on a stretcher, babbling o' green fields.

Now, if what you have had published is a work of substance, such as new clinical evidence that human sperm have started swimming in circles, your promotional interview with a media person can be relatively stress-free as you parrot replies to the same questions while holding the same courtesy cup of degenerate coffee. No problem.

However, if you are tagged as having written humour, spun fluff, the interviewer has no hook on which to hang attention. He or she, therefore, expects the humorist to be funny into a microphone that rears like a cobra ready to strike, or under television studio lights that turn the effects of his sleepless night into the picture of Dorian Gray, latter phase.

Now, it is a fact of anthropology that the professional humorist is never amusing when there is no money in it. It goes against his principles, like a priest acting pious on a Saturday. Even that more gregarious form of humorist, the stand-up comedian, is notorious for being sullen once he sits down. True to form, I have disappointed countless

"Of course! I'd be delighted to inscribe a personal message to your Uncle Fred and . . ." (BCBW)

hostesses at parties by being totally jokeless, with the mien of a basset hound with the gout.

Among the other hard lessons I've learned during the course of flogging a book:

1. It is useless to wear a clown's nose when being interviewed on radio.

2. To be photographed holding a copy of your book under your chin, while you expose your teeth, will cause all your body hair to fall off.

3. Book promotion on television is the other profession where you put on a lot of makeup and expose yourself in public.

4. The talk show host will not have read your book, and will need to refer to a piece of paper to remember your name.

5. Do not check your zipper if you are already on camera.

6. Pancake, when applied by a makeup girl who has had a long day, can work into your eyes and turn the whole interview into a pitch for the CNIB.

7. Preparing your ad-libs in advance of your interview is an isometric exercise in futility.

8. There is one question you can expect to be asked on an average of 379 times per promotion tour: "Where do you get your ideas?" Reply: "I get mine from a short, fat guy who hangs around the steam bath smoking a cigar." I have never used this answer, being guts challenged.

The crown jewel of comedown in an author's book promotion is without question the autographing party. One of the myths of the trade—sedulously nurtured by publishers— is that the autographing party gives the author the thrill of mass adulation, up close and personal, from hordes of book buyers lined up for hours for the privilege of having a title page inscribed by the demigod behind the desk.

Don't eat that, Elmer.

It may hold for celebrities like O.J. Simpson, who have been tried for murder, or for a former Canadian prime minister such as Pierre Trudeau, but if all the author has done is write, the autographing party is apt to make Robinson Crusoe's desert isle look like a Boxing Day sale at Sears.

The autographing party is arranged by the publisher's agent, usually an attractive young woman whom I try to persuade to forget the whole mission and run away with me to Samoa. She rarely yields. Instead I am picked up by her tumbrel and delivered to a series of bookstores and department stores where the manager has: (1) forgotten I was scheduled to come; (2) not yet unpacked the four copies of my book that she ordered; or (3) set up a card table for me in the window so that the entire world can observe, in passing, the spectacle of a man motionless enough to be a men's wear mannequin, except for the mismatched socks.

Autographing in a department store books section invites a few additional punches to the *amour propre*. Mind you, I have come to expect that no one will come up to me except the beer-breath geezer who asks, "Where's the washroom?" I'm happy to direct him into the wilds of women's lingerie, where he may disgrace himself in style. I see it as a public service.

A more bitter pill was the autographing I was once lured into doing near the furniture department of The Bay in downtown Vancouver. The books manager had set up the utility table but, unable to find a stool for me, borrowed a rather handsome armchair from the nearby array of home furnishings. As usual I couldn't draw flies until a little old lady came up to where I was sitting.

"Hi!" I said, pen poised for the first sale of the day.

The LOL ignored this overture, adjusting her glasses to get a better squint at the price tag on the leg of my chair. Then she rasped at me, "Would you mind getting out of the chair?"

"Not at all," I said, minding plenty but getting up.

While I stood by, the LOL eased herself into the chair, jiggled her bottom to test the upholstery, considered the back support and finally stood out of my seat. Giving me a black look, she snapped, "It's overpriced." And she toddled off.

Afterward I cursed myself for not giving her a reduced price on the chair, taking cash and getting the hell out of there.

So, if I have a message for aspiring authors—and, as you

suspected, I do—it is this: forget it, unless you have the stamina of a cross-Channel swimmer and the sensitivity of a used-car dealer. A thick skin, to match the leather of your luggage that fails to come down the airport carousel, is a must.

Today book promotion will weed you out, with cold-blooded Darwinism, if you are sickly or cry easily. Pale, TB-ridden John Keats would never have made it to the bestseller list if he hadn't been lucky enough to live before the book promotion tour took over from service on a galley ship. Choose a professional athlete as your role model. Ken Dryden, for example, needed his career as a hockey goalie to condition him, mentally and physically, for the rigours of flacking for his books.

Does this make writing a young man's game? No, more of a young woman's game. Women are the sturdier gender, for this as for most other pursuits that require getting out of bed in the morning. Male authors should plan to retire at forty before they lose it in the legs.

Chapter 21

Maybe a Life
Too Literal

hen the *Province* retired me at sixty-five, I
put in a special request: please don't give me
a piece of luggage as my going-away present.

I had worked long enough—thirty-five years—at the paper
to have attended a lot of retirement parties in the cafeteria,
and seen the retiree handed a piece of luggage. It was as if
the company wanted to make sure he would go a long, long
way away before realizing his pension wouldn't cover it.

"Enjoy that escorted tour of Afghanistan," they seemed to
say, "and here is something to carry your personal effects
when they're returned to your next of kin."

When my turn came, I had no urge to rediscover the
romance of amoebic dysentery. I let it be known that what I
really would like was a telescope. Astronomy had always
attracted me because, like writing, it is something you can

do lying down. And what is humour but looking at things through the wrong end of the telescope?

Management grumbled, having its heart set on retiring me with a suitcase, but did give me a cheque to cover the telescope. I bought a beaut—not as fancy as the Mount Palomar model, but my entrée to awe-inspiring sights until the lady across the lane bought venetian blinds.

Anyway, I don't need a magnifying lens to look back on my life. I can see the craters on *that* moon. Hey, if astronomers have found life on Mars, maybe someone should take another look at *my* X-rays.

Not that my life was dead. I did have my moments. None come to mind right now, but maybe that's why I don't feel guilt. It is easier to be guilt-free when, like me, you're a devout determinist. Whatever I have done, nature plus nurture made me do it. I accept no responsibility. Mind you, seeing Lady Luck as the Goddess of Everything does have its downside: I can take pride in nothing. It's a sort of low-grade humility.

I have played the hand that was dealt me and was fortunate enough to have been in the bathroom when the saloon got shot up.

On a different level of contrition, I hate to think that my surviving as a professional humorist may have encouraged other people to try to make a living at it. When I talk to creative writing classes, or to high school students keen to avoid real work by writing humour, I always give them the same advice: slash your wrists now before the arteries harden.

Not that I regret playing the Fool. The Fool is the only person in court who gets to sit in the presence of the king or queen. True, he has to sit on the floor. But for someone with a bad back it beats standing around and waiting for your turn to kiss the royal ass.

Woody Allen has given us his assessment of our status: "When you write comedy, you are put at the children's table. When you write tragedy, you eat with the adults." If, indeed, you eat at all. That depends, more and more, on whether you write comedy for television and movies, move to Hollywood and get both a good agent and a good treatment for stomach ulcers. But the print humorist is an endangered species. Every year I expect to receive a Canadian Wildlife Federation calendar with my picture on it.

Still undaunted? Okay, check us out in any bookstore. You will find that the humour section is at the back beside the books for mentally challenged children.

Do I have any regrets? You didn't ask, but I'll tell you, anyway. Woody Allen has also said that his only regret is that he was not someone else. Besides regretting that I was not Woody Allen, I regret that I never learned how to swim. Swimming is one of the few physical pleasures one can enjoy in old age. Even just floating in a pool with pretty women in skimpy bikinis can be stimulating. But I never recovered from my first swimming lesson. Please let me lie on the couch here, Doctor, and talk about it.

My mother took me, aged about five, to the Crystal Pool, Vancouver's only indoor saltwater bathing facility, to join a class of other shivering fry. From the moment of having to disrobe in public and walk barefoot through a trough of greenish disinfectant as though my feet were mobile fungus, my attitude toward natation was negative. I descended gingerly into the pool, chivvied by an instructor smart enough not to immerse *him*self in water treated with an unknown quantity of nervous piddle.

"When I blow the whistle," the instructor bellowed, "I want you all to take a deep breath and duck your head right under the water for as long as you can. Okay?" Phweep!

I took a deep breath. Then I looked down at the water right under my chin and saw a large bumblebee doing the deadman's float right where I was supposed to duck my head. I had to make a quick decision. My decision was to climb out of the pool, get dressed and go home with my mother, who was in no mood to discuss the bumblebee's right-of-way in a public pool.

I didn't make another attempt to learn to swim until I was in my fifties. No joy. What I learned was that it is very dangerous for a known humorist to enter water more than ankle-deep, because those watching assume he is simulating drowning just to get a laugh.

Another regret: I sometimes wish that, just once in my life, I had got drunk, if only to compare it with other ways of falling down. Nor have I ever sniffed, snorted, smoked or shot up any hallucinogenic except the stock market. My consciousness has never been raised. It has just lain there for all these years like the *Titanic*. Hardly worth raising now, wedged as it is in reality.

Fact is, in the feast of life, I have been a digestive biscuit. I may have been overly concerned about remaining alive. While I don't think I am a bona fide coward, I concede that I view being courageous as something of a last resort. To me the inevitability of death is one more thing to be avoided.

The only time I have sought to live dangerously is in my sex fantasies. When I was young, the most adventurous of these was that of being trapped by a blizzard in a hunter's cabin, alone with a beautiful, half-breed nymphomaniac who was well supplied with a bearskin rug, a leghold trap, a leather harness, an eclectic selection of whips and thirty feet of logging chain. When I was about fifty, the blizzard abated. We had a chinook. A few years later the beautiful half-breed was miraculously cured of her morbid hypersex-

Sitting on my laurels, 1995, with perfect teeth to spit a curve (1995). Eat your heart out, Woody.

uality. I became sensitive to her ethnic problems, and we spent more time wandering in the woods, admiring moss. After I turned seventy, the young lady left the cabin to go home and take care of her aging father, and the cabin was demolished to make a retirement home with cute nurses.

A final regret: none of my fantasies have been of the spiritual type. Despite being a determinist, I could have done with a shot of religious ecstasy, something to reduce my philosophical dependency on the fortuitous. But the only time I have felt close to Jesus was when I was a kid, feeling sorry for him because his birthday, like mine (December 28), was so close to Christmas. I knew he wouldn't get many birthday presents, since people combined them with Christmas gifts under the one-tree-fits-all-occasions. His mother, Mary, said to him, "Jesus, dear, half of this bottle of myrrh is from Santa, and the other half is for your birthday."

Now that I am of an age to regard birthday presents with the fish-eye, I pay more attention to one of the larger truths of Christ's teaching. Which is: the best social-security system is love. Unless our love is like a 7-Eleven, the heart open twenty-four hours a day, all the presents in the world won't keep a family in business.

At seventy-eight (PST) I have lived longer than I expected. If whom the gods love die young, I seem to have offended them. I may well see the arrival of the millennium, a fanciful idea for someone with a history of custard pie.

By rights, I should have been snuffed in World War II, as were some of my classmates in high school, whose children today would have been dying to own a German BMW or a Japanese Lexus. (Sorry, it just slipped out.)

My excuse for living: maybe laughter *is* the best medicine. And if so, I hope that you, dear reader, have been taking your medication.